Table Of Contents

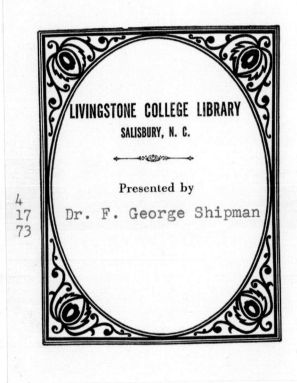

PREFACE

The Study of Religion in the Undergraduate Curriculum is an outgrowth of a long-standing concern by the Association of American Colleges' Commission on Religion in Higher Education to encourage and improve the study of religion as an academic discipline in all undergraduate liberal arts colleges. The study, directed by Claude Welch, formerly Chairman of the Department of Religious Thought at the University of Pennsylvania and now Dean of the Graduate Theological Union at Berklely, California, represents an impressive compilation, analysis, and interpretation of current practices and experimental efforts at the undergraduate level.

Over the past half dozen years considerable attention has been devoted to the study of religion in American colleges and universities by various concerned groups. Two particularly noteworthy reports are *The Study of Religion in American Universities* (1965), authored by Robert Michaelson and sponsored by the Society for Religion in Higher Education, and *The Study of Religion on the Campus of Today* (1967), a selection of papers from a conference sponsored by the Association of American Colleges edited by Carl D. Hartzell and Harrison Sasscer.

In 1969 the American Council of Learned Societies undertook a study of graduate education in the field of religion. This study produced a wealth of comprehensive information on the current status and format of undergraduate programs in religion at over 800 colleges and universities. Recognizing the value of this information, the Commission on Religion in Higher Education of the AAC resolved to seek foundation support to enable it to utilize this data in a separate study of religion in undergraduate programs.

The purpose of such a study was three-fold: (1) to describe and analyze existing undergraduate programs in religion; (2) to describe and analyze new curricular developments and experimental efforts in the field, and (3) to present various perspectives on the undergraduate teaching of religion. The completed study is addressed to those constituencies inside and outside our colleges and universities who are concerned with the teaching of religion — academic administrators, faculties of religion, religious communities and church boards of higher education.

The Edward W. Hazen Foundation and the National Endowment for the Humanities generously responded to our request for funds to support this project, and to both of these philanthropic organizations the Association is most grateful. It is our hope that the information gathered in this study will contribute to a continuing dialogue on the role of the teaching of religion as an academic discipline.

Samuel H. Magill
Executive Associate
Association of American Colleges

Part I
Points of View

Campus Ministry and Its Relationship To Religious Studies

Beverly A. Asbury

To one who is a practicing campus minister, this topic has many personal dimensions. To one who still "preaches", in both formal and personal ways, it is natural not only to begin with a personal dimension but also with a homiletical (and in this instance, authentic) example.

The setting was a January day in another state.

I had been away from my home base on a professional errand, and I was now returning. Getting to the airport had been a hassle. Freezing rain had been falling for nearly a day. The forecasted thaw had not arrived. The airlines nevertheless said that one should come on to the airport. So, by the hardest, there I was, and I joined the long line at the ticket counter, keeping an eye on the outside conditions.

It became evident that no flights would be landing, and before my turn at the counter came, fly-overs were being announced. Planes could still take off but could not land there. It appeared that I might be stranded in a crowded airport lobby, but I had noticed one plane already parked at Gate 3. I asked the agent where that plane was going and if there were seats available on it. Yes, space was available, and although the plane's destination was out of my way a bit, it would provide a connection home free of bad weather.

Re-ticketed and relieved, I clambered aboard and plopped my exhausted body in a seat. In the adjacent seat was an old friend, who had become a professor of religion in a fine university. We were astonished and pleased to see each other and to have a chance to talk. We shared a common past, had taken somewhat different turns in life, but we had continued a relationship of mutual trust and affection.

Our conversation soon turned to professional matters, and we spoke of the rather sorry state of the institutional church and the paucity of good preaching. We talked of the ministerial identity crisis and of the "house divided" between "liberals" and "conservatives." We moved to a discussion of what had happened to the old "certainties", the dogmas and beliefs within which we had been raised and within whose context we had received a neo-orthodox theological education. Our analyses were remarkably similar, and we agreed that the religious situation was marked with great un-

Beverly A. Asbury is University Chaplain/Director of Religious Affairs, Vanderbilt University.

certainty and a clouded future, nowhere more acutely evident than in the contemporary university scene.

At this point and without condescension, my friend indicated that he really felt sorry for me and others still involved in ministry, in the practice of religion, especially on a university campus. With genuine regard, he indicated his feeling that it must be tough indeed trying to minister during a period of such uncertainty and transition. It occurred to me that the plight of the minister at this point was really the plight of anyone trying to determine his priorities and act them out when the historic foundations have been so shaken and are still shaking. I then asked him how he dealt with the problem.

He replied that his situation was different, that he did not have to deal with it in the same sense. He said that he was a professional student of religion, an observer, a teacher. He would, he said, study men like me and all the phenomena in our day, but there was no personal trauma or anxiety in the situation for him.

This recollection may be incomplete, distorted, and unfair. But it is a remembrance. It left me dissatisfied as a personal statement. It may have produced some envy that I didn't have the credentials myself to move outside the ministry and become an objective, dispassionate, and even casual observer of religion. However, most of all, it characterized one of the differences between those who minister and "practice" religion on our college and university campuses and those who teach about religion there.

This is not to say that those who teach religion do not practice religion or do not have the personal dimensions of religion present in their lives. Of course they do—even my friend on the plane ride can't completely escape the struggles of doubt and belief, faith and unfaith, certainty and skepticism. Both Robert Bellah and Peter Slater elsewhere in this book state that they both have clearly revealed their own religious commitments. Both also maintain that there are important reasons for doing so in their classes. Nevertheless, there is truly a great professional difference between the minister who serves and represents a particular religious tradition and the scientific investigator and scholarly professor of the various religious traditions. The professional and even personal fate of the former is far more related to the historical circumstances of a given religious tradition than it is for the latter. Whatever the minister's intellectual acumen and professional training, insofar as he is a practitioner of religion, a servant of it, and not primarily a student of it, he has a greater stake in the health and welfare of that tradition. Whatever the critical distance from his tradition possessed by the minister, he cannot as minister-qua-minister possess the objectivity and emotional detachment of the teacher of religion and still fulfill the historic functions of ministry. Obviously, neither the teacher nor the minister can or would deny or disguise the genuine differences.

4

These differences between the minister and teacher of religion have been stated a number of ways, and most of those ways result in oversimplifications and distortions. For example, one way of posing the differences lies in talking about the affective aspects of religion as over against the cognitive aspects. While that can be a helpful functional distinction, it becomes a perversion when pushed so far as to make it appear that ministry never relates to cognitive aspects and that teaching never touches upon the affective. Or, to put it another way, the campus minister would never want to concede that the practice of religion precludes the objective study of religion, and the professor of religion would surely hold that this study of religion neither rules out nor compels any given practice of religion. In short, a neat bifurcation does not and cannot exist. Yet, despite the inadequacies present in any statement of the differences, the differences are there; they are real, and there are many practical and political reasons why the practice of religion and the teaching of religion should be separated, distanced from each other, however much they are related.

Other chapters develop what those reasons are. Among them on the academic side are the need for scholarly inquiry and teaching to be independent of the elements of "creed, code, and cult" (Slater); the need to establish academic (secular) respectability; and the need to relate to the other academic disciplines in the university. One might say that objectivity, "coolness," critical distance are essential in the teaching of religion.

On the ministerial side, commitment and action would be considered more essential. The minister, the practitioner of religion, on a college campus is concerned not merely with content, inquiry, and rational analysis. He is also bound to be professionally concerned with persons, feelings, relationships, values, conduct, ritual expressions, prophetic utterances and actions. The campus minister's concerns are not unrelated to the academic enterprise, and he increasingly feels that many religious programs should be considered to be "co-curricula" rather than "extra-curricula," indicating that religion and its practice are not anti-intellectual and that the university is an important place for working out religious commitments. Even so, the minister on campus is not primarily concerned with the curricula, the academic, but with personal and social religious expression. Indeed, the minister involved with liturgy, with the work of a religious people, knows that action is necessary and that he must be free to apologize for it, advocate it, and involve himself in it apart from scholarly considerations. He is even likely to maintain that a religious man need not and cannot wait "until all the evidence is in" before acting on his convictions, however that scandalizes his academic colleague.

These differences have often created a deep sense of mistrust and even dislike between campus ministers and teachers of religion on the same campus and far more generally. Campus ministers have often felt that much of the teaching of religion took forms irrelevant to the practice of religion, and, indeed, never seemed to produce people who had convictions on which to act. Beyond that, campus ministers of conservative or fundamentalist persuasions have looked upon the teaching of religion as inimical to the best interests of their religious tradition. They have looked upon the classroom as the stronghold of the "enemy" — the place where "true belief" was undermined, where "faith" was "destroyed." This still continues, and one wonders if it is not likely to have a resurgence. That is, liberal religion seems, for a moment anyway, to be on the decline, but there has been no corresponding setback for the more conservative religious establishment. Furthermore, pietistic and literalistic developments among young people outside all religious institutions could indicate future strength among those critical and fearful of the teaching of religion. Of course, they may stay away from course work in religion altogether, leaving the field to others both inside and outside religious institutions who have more esoteric and less institutional interest in religion.

The negative attitude toward the teaching of religion is neither new nor restricted to certain sectarian groups. The original impetus for campus ministries was colored by an anti-intellectual and anti-university attitude in the churches. Many early efforts to provide campus ministries intended to provide a "home away from home" for the students of particular religious and denominational commitments (which were generally one and the same). Some campus ministries still continue this thrust, building "student centers" for their constituencies, speaking of "student work," and basically ignoring if not resisting the larger university setting and all for which it stands. Such ministries are motivated, at least in part, by the desire to protect students from the threat of the university's intellectual and social challenge to their religious tradition. Success in such ministries would mean returning the students to their homes with their "beliefs" intact, albeit better informed and more articulate about them. The university has been a hurdle successfully negotiated.

Other evolving campus ministries have differed greatly from that model and have developed significant theologies for life and work in the colleges and universities. They have seen the university as an ally and have encouraged students to engage in religious studies. Where departments of religious studies have not previously existed, some of these campus ministers have been active in encouraging their establishment. Often, in the period of a college's life when no academic courses in religion were offered, campus ministries themselves provided such courses. Some colleges even allowed elective credit for these "off-campus" courses and recognized "Bible chairs" that existed in denominational centers.

As that period ended, campus ministers learned to support the university-qua-university and not merely its teaching of religion.

The theology of these more liberal ministries touted the university as the central institution of our culture, *the* place in which to work out the role of religious commitment in human life. Those campus ministers who were committed to the reformation of the church envisioned the university to be *the* place from which that job could best begin. Those who desired to reform American society as well also saw the university as the beginning place. Even when disillusionment set in about church reform, there was still faith in the university's role in American social reformation. In any event, many involved in campus ministry believed that theirs was not only a specialized ministry of the church but perhaps its most significant and important ministry, given the centrality of the university in American society.

They also looked upon the university as their "home" and upon those teaching religion as their colleagues, if not their allies. If they grew alienated from anything, it was the church and not the university. Indeed, the university often became their "church." Most of them had long since discovered the faults and wrongheadedness of religion and its institutions. It may be that these campus ministers had gained a critical distance from the church but too simply endorsed the academic institutions in which they labored. A more adequate theology or even a sociology of institutions might have prepared them to find that the university had many of the same faults as the church. When they discovered that it did, many of these same campus ministers adopted a program of "reforming the university" not unakin to their previous program of "reforming the church." In this they discovered themselves entirely without an *institutional* constituency, having already given up on one and now being disillusioned with the other. Moreover, when experience taught them that the university was at least as intractable and as resistant to change and reformation as the church, some of these campus ministers in their new and deeper disillusionment turned on the university with a vengeance. Alienated now from both church and university, some found a new constituency with the "radicals" attacking the university as the first step in a new American "revolution." Perhaps their own "belief" in the centrality of the university made them susceptible to radical rhetoric about the "university as the engine of society." It's an easy step from one inflated view of the university to another inflated view of it, and several prominent campus ministers took it in the late 1960's and led others to take it. In this process, these campus ministers gave up on religion and its ministry and on the university and its teaching— even its teaching of religion, perhaps most on its teaching of religion.

Fortunately, not all outside the more conservative campus ministries have gone that way. Others are regrouping, reexamining their theologies, reworking their definitions and relationships. Of course, they are doing so in the face of many suspicions and hostilities. The church has become as skeptical of its representatives on the campus as those representatives have long been of the church, and now the church faces a deepening crisis anyway. In a drive to reallocate diminishing financial resources, the campus ministries have been drastically reduced or even eliminated from church budgets. At the same time, the university faces its own crises of finances and meaning and function. It has grown wary of campus ministers because of the awareness that some of them have exacerbated tensions and conflicts within the university. Some people within both the church and the university would look with pleasure on the demise of campus ministries. There may even be a tendency to look upon new models of work and creative moves toward ecumenical and inter-faith ministries as signs of weakness more than anything else. However, precisely those ministries are developing an alternative model for the future on campus and elsewhere and at a time when religious interest seems to be rising in America's youth culture.

Indeed, those new and developing ministries may be the only ministries equipped to relate to the religious interest of America's youth, insofar as the university continues to be their cultural home. But they surely cannot do so oblivious to those who are engaged in the teaching of religion, and they will not seek to do so. They are also now in a better position to develop new relationships there. For one thing, the new models of campus ministry are neither anti-intellectual nor anti-university. Within the framework of religious commitments, they possess a critical distance from both religious establishments of "creed, code, and cult" as well as a critical distance from the academic institutions which are now seen to have their own "creeds, codes, and cults." They are prepared to work out new relationships with those involved in the teaching structures of the university and to engage themselves in specialized and functional ministries to all those who are involved in the higher education "community." That is, these ministries which transcend many of the old lines of "creed, code, and cult" no longer possess deep distrust of their academic colleagues, and they hope to overcome whatever distrust is felt toward them.

Those engaged in ecumenical and inter-faith ministries, in ministries of functional specialization, understand that academic religious studies can be and generally are responsible to the religious communities as well as to the university community. These ministries would never expect and, indeed, would oppose any teaching of religion that had a propagandistic or apologetic basis. Therefore, they endorse the academic study of religion wherever it is objective, fair, and representative of the religion being taught and of the whole range of religious expression. And it generally is!

Campus ministers, men and women engaged in leading those seeking to practice religion on campus, increasingly recognize the integrity, intelligence, and skill of those involved in scientific inves-

8

tigation, scholarly inquiry, and teaching of religion. They have often been helped themselves by the teachers of religion in understanding themselves and their professional work, and they would seek to support and defend the value of religious studies, their independence and academic integrity.

The development of academic departments of religion, as stated earlier, can now be seen by emerging ministries as not only strengthening their work but also freeing them from certain teaching functions performed in the past for which they were not necessarily prepared. Where adequate departments of religious studies exist, campus ministries do not have to use their resources to develop teaching structures and, of course, should never do so in a parallel way. In other words, the existence of faculties in religious studies frees campus ministers to develop the historical modalities of pastoral and priestly ministry, governance, and prophetic inquiry in new ways appropriate to the emerging university situation.

At another level, religious studies have aided the process of removing sectarian expression from much of campus ministry's work, a key development in preparing them for ministry to the contemporary youth culture. Naturally, other factors have also been present in that—the rise of religious syncretism and new interest in astrology, magic, primitive ritual, nature, celebration, etc. In some respects religious studies have aided those developments too and in other respects undercut them or made them reflective. However, insofar as they have helped students to learn to analyze and assess commitments, they have helped produce a new situation for campus ministries. That is, campus ministers cannot, for the most part, any longer assume a denominational constituency. Students no longer identify religiously because of birth or earlier training. Institutional religion and its influence have declined precisely at the time when there has been a great expansion of departments of religious studies and a rise in the religious interest of students, albeit an unconventional, non-institutional interest.

The move away from sectarianism and to ecumenical ministries is fraught with dangers if not "heresies." In an attempt to attract youth, to be "with it," to overcome ministerial and ecclesiastical identity crises, campus ministers face the danger of becoming dilettantes, jumping from cause to cause, fad to fad, etc. However important it may be to alter perceptions and perspectives, nothing would be gained by such a development. There is no reason why ecumenical and inter-faith developments have to be at the expense of the integrity of historical traditions, and much can be learned by a study of religious development in other periods of our history. In these matters, campus ministers have learned to look to those in religious studies for help. At other times, with help unsought, they have felt critical stings from the teachers of religion. In many ways, campus ministers have felt the presence and influence of their teaching colleagues.

For their own part, those in religious studies have begun developing a new appreciation of the campus ministers. While they have had to overcome the suspicions mentioned earlier, they have witnessed the professional developments in campus ministry and have included the growing literature from it and about it in some of their studies. The professors of religion seem now to recognize the integrity of campus ministry and its new independence of the sectarian aspects of "creed, code, and cult." One reason for this lies in the fact that those campus ministries which survived the last decade demonstrate a responsibility to the university community while not idolizing it any longer. Campus ministries no longer beholden simply to the religious community and professors of religious studies responsible to the religious as well as to the university community have a new point of beginning. The practitioners (?) of religion and the teachers of religion have overlapping communities. Priorities and degrees of loyalty differ, but they can no longer ignore their common responsibilities and interests.

This is not to hold that role differentiations will blur or disappear. They should not and will not. Indeed, they can best serve each other by maintaining a "critical distance" from each other.

Experience has taught the campus minister to keep his distance not only from the church but also from the university. It has become a keystone of campus ministry theology to be in but not of the university. By keeping a critical distance, the practitioners of religion on campus can analyze and criticize the "creed, code, and cult" of the university, examining presuppositions, and revealing commitments where none allegedly exist. The hidden commitments of academic pursuits, the strange bifurcations between teaching, research, policy, and action must surely be of interest to a minister who seeks to locate and explicate the "meaning of things."

Religion has to do with these commitments, world-views, "creeds, codes, and cults." Continuing conversations between those who lead in campus religious expressions and those who study and teach religion about these are necessary and would be illuminating. Ministers can provide experiential data and scholars can provide a framework of analysis. Scholars may have to reexamine presumed boundaries and deal with previously unobserved religious phenomena. Both may grow in understanding how and why men are religious in our time, especially with the life of the university.

A particular reason for keeping distance from the university lies in the continuing need to place before the academics the insistence that religion is more than subject matter and, especially, that religion's transcendental dimension be not ignored. While campus ministers have no objection to and do endorse the value of the humanistic and scientific study of religion, their distance allows them to insist that there is more, that having learned all there is to know about religion, a religious man is more than he knows. Or, to put it another way, the distance from the university enables the campus minister to discern reductionism, expose it, and resist it — and by so doing, hopefully both open a dialogue and defend religious expression for what it is and must be.

One additional reason for critical distance from the university lies in ministry's calling to combine inquiry and action. There is little reason to think that the university can or will become an "actor" in social reform, quite apart from the debate over whether it *should* be or not. However, Western religious traditions, at least, insist that religious convictions and personal and social action have an inextricable relationship. Prophetic advocacy and action, therefore, are very much a part of ministry, and while the university can and should "inform" such advocacy and action, it should not determine its appropriateness or content.

"*In* but *not of*" the university leaves campus ministry free to adopt new strategies, to make independent judgments on the basis of its own commitments, to say "no" to its "friends" when they're "wrong" and "yes" to its "enemies" when they're "right." Campus ministry can help the teachers of religion — now insisting to the teachers that religious studies are directly related to the student's "creed, code, and cult;" then urging the students to study religion before expressing uncritical beliefs or engaging in unexamined practices; now asking faculty to counsel their students in a broader than academic framework; then referring students to professors for counseling in religious content; now assuring the teacher of religion that his lack of classroom advocacy does not make him suspect in the religious communities; then insisting to the critics that advocacy is not an academic function but a ministerial, ecclesiastic, or personal one.

More could be said, surely, but these suggestions, "hints," directions will suffice. Less needs to be said about the critical distance teachers of religion must have from the religious communities. For one thing, they ought to and have said that for themselves. For another, that is largely *fait accompli*, and campus ministers today would never expect or ask that it be surrendered. It has been too dearly won and remains too important to be sacrificed for any reason. It does not necessitate mutual suspicion and it does not prevent respect and cooperation but rather forms its basis.

As religious studies and campus ministries know each other better and grow in mutual respect, campus ministries will benefit from the academic critique of their priorities and the adequacy and relevance of them. Campus ministries will also find it less likely that they will wish to restore their sectarian perspectives and more difficult to do so if they try. Campus ministries will certainly learn more and more from the teachers about the diversity and plurality of religions and the relativism of all religions and hopefully learn more about their own religious commitments and practices.

For campus ministry's part, there is no doubt about the possibilities and values of better relationships to those engaged in teaching religion. We can learn more from each other than either is presently aware. I, for one, anyway, have a better idea of what to pursue the next time I find myself on a plane next to a professor of religion. The agenda is clear, compelling, and appealing. Indeed, I don't intend to wait for a plane ride. Some of the teachers are right next door.

Religion in the University:
Changing Consciousness,
Changing Structures

Robert N. Bellah

As this volume richly documents, the department of religion has emerged in the American university as a place for the study of the whole range of man's religions, including especially oriental religions, with a wide range of theoretical and methodological approaches, including especially those of the social sciences: anthropology, sociology, and psychology. In these respects it differs markedly from the traditional seminary curriculum. But in the degree to which it takes seriously the existential questions with which religion deals and attempts to attain a sympathetic understanding of the meaning of different religious symbol systems, the department of religion is not wholly in accord with the dominant ethos of the secular university either. Both seminary and secular university have looked askance at this emerging structure for the study of religion and some individuals from both have tried to obstruct or minimize the general acceptance of the department of religion as a valid intellectual enterprise. Such opposition is not altogether misguided. The department of religion as it has taken shape, particularly in the last ten years, represents a form of religious consciousness not wholly reconcilable with that of the traditional seminary or the secular university. Although the three forms of religious consciousness arose successively, they are all alive and healthy at the present time and will probably survive for an indefinite time to come. It would be well to examine the implications of these three forms of religious consciousness for the study of religion, since many of the controversies concerning the department of religion in the university arise from conflicts between them, not least from unresolved conflicts between members of the department of religion themselves. It might facilitate discussion to begin with a brief tabular presentation of the three types:

Type of Religious Consciousness	Attitude toward Religion	Educational Structure
1. Religious orthodoxy	Primary naivete	Seminary
2. Enlightenment orthodoxy	Criticism (scepticism)	Secular University
3. Symbolic realism	Second naivete	Department of Religion

Robert N. Bellah is Ford Professor of Sociology and Comparative Studies and Director of the Center for Japanese and Korean Studies, University of California, Berkeley.

Perhaps the best way to differentiate the three types is to see how they view the crucial problem of religious pluralism. Most men have been in some sense religious, but they have had a great variety of religions. Traditional religion has held that there is only one true religion and all the others are false, or if not absolutely false, at least represent lower levels of spiritual understanding than that of the true religion. Stated in this way not only Western religions that tended to view other religions as the work of the devil but Eastern religions as well shared this view, for the latter, in spite of their greater "tolerance," showed an inveterate proclivity to rank religious systems in such a way as to prove that one's own was at the apex of religious understanding.

The secular enlightenment saw religious diversity as one (among many others) proof of the illusory nature of all religions. Indeed the bizarre diversity of cults and sects became itself a point of ridicule in the rationalist critique of religions, and it was a point of honor for rationalist scholars to show that Judaism and Christianity were no less outlandish than the religion of the heathen Chinese, and maybe more so. Even among those scholars who showed no polemic hostility, a gentle irony toward all the wayward phantasms of the human mind was not uncommon. Secure in their rational understanding of the universe and man, such scholars looked on religion as a curious museum within which to study the abberations of the human spirit.

There is no question but that great scholarly contributions to the understanding of religion have been made by scholars with both these points of view. In fact the study of religion is largely indebted to such men, the achievements of those who share the third type of consciousness being as yet incipient. For the latter all religions are to be taken seriously but no one of them is held absolute. For the religiously orthodox religious belief systems were felt to represent "objective" reality as it really is, and thus if one of them is true the owners must be false, either absolutely or in some degree. For the secular orthodox all religion is merely "subjective," based on emotion, wish or faulty inference, and therefore false. For the third group, who take symbolism seriously, religion is seen as a system of symbols which is neither simply objective nor simply subjective but which links subject and object in a way that transfigures reality or even, in a sense, creates reality. For people with this point of view the idea of finding more than one religion valid, even in a deeply personal sense, is not only possible but normal. This means neither syncretism nor relativism, since it is possible within any social or personal context to develop criteria for the evaluation of religious phenomena and a consequent hierarchy of choices. But the entire range of man's spiritual experiences, for such people, is personally, existentially, available.

I don't want to push this schema very hard, least of all to argue that the position of symbolic realism as I have just described it is a necessary prerequisite for a department of religion or for members of it. Those committed to religious orthodoxy and to enlightenment orthodoxy still have much to contribute to such departments provided their scholarship is competent. But I sense that the third position is the commonest and has the easiest fit in at least some of the newer more innovative departments. Since I feel the third position is a valid one, and indeed one that has much to contribute both to education and to modern culture generally, I think it is worth making it explicit and, if need be, defending it against attack.[1]

I have singled out the emphasis on oriental religions and on social science as especially significant in the emergence of the department of religion with its incipient new consciousness. Perhaps it is worth exploring why these two emphases seem strategic. One way of handling man's religious diversity that appealed in the 19th century to both the religious and the enlightenment orthodox was to cast it in some evolutionary form showing that Christianity is the "highest" religion or that science is the most advanced form of human thought to which religion is merely an inadequate precursor. But as Western knowledge of oriental religions deepened and the range of spiritual insight in Hinduism, Buddhism, Taoism and Confucianism came to be better appreciated, it was not so obvious that these systems were "inferior" to Christianity, nor, among many who had discovered that science is a useful method for the understanding of a restricted range of problems but a most inadequate total world-view, to science either. At a period when primitive and archaic religions were still being treated with considerable condescension, it became impossible to look down on the thought of a Chuang Tzu or a Shankara. It was in confrontation with the profounder expressions of oriental religion, I would suggest, that the radical pluralism (not the same thing as relativism) of the third form of religious consciousness first began to develop. It is certainly true that until rather recently, when primitive and archaic religions have begun to seem equally accessible, it was the teaching of oriental religions that most readily communicated this radical pluralism to students. Of course what was being understood was someone else's "religious orthodoxy," and that involved a good deal more than sympathy and good vibrations. A great deal of very hard work by orientalists, many of whom were orthodox Christians or secular sceptics, was required to unlock the books and trace the traditions which would allow us to see the eastern religions, at least in part, from the "inside." But when that work had been in good part achieved we were in a new situation religiously, a situation without any but very partial and sporadic precedent in earlier human history.

It is my belief, however, that the full implications of the increasing availability of the oriental religions even in part to our "inner" experience would not have been drawn had not the developments in oriental studies been complemented by developments

15

in the social sciences. This latter development was if anything even more unexpected than the consequences of the achievements of oriental studies since the social scientific study of religion had begun almost exclusively from a position of enlightenment orthodoxy in which the chief aim of the enterprise was to explain religion away as the consequence of certain economic, social or psychological variables. It is certainly true that many social scientists continue with this enterprise as originally conceived but I have argued elsewhere that in the work of the most profound and original social scientists, Freud, Weber and Durkheim, as developed by at least some of their successors what has been paradoxically discovered in the indelibly religious basis of all social and personal existence.[2] Thus religion, far from being an outmoded symbolic form, proves to be generic to the human species and as such an essential key to the understanding of man. But this position, while ending up reasserting the centrality of religion that traditional cultures had proclaimed, denied the absolutism of orthodoxy by insisting on taking with equal seriousness the entire range of man's religiousness. It has become part, I think, of the teaching of many departments of religion that religion is deeply rooted in the most basic structure of man's personality, society and culture. It is no accident, I think, that many of those most influential in the field of religious studies today have been influenced both by oriental studies and by social science: Mircea Eliade, Norman O. Brown, Herbert Fingarette, Paul Ricoeur.[3]

There is perhaps some relation between my third form of religious consciousness and what is loosely called the counter-culture or indeed Charles Reich's Consciousness III. The developments leading to the emergence of this kind of religious consciousness undoubtedly contributed to and were to some degree facilitated by the cultural effervescence of the last ten years. But what I am referring to goes deeper, both in time and in seriousness, than most of the counter-culture. Much of the current fad of oriental religions in the United States is not so much the opening up of new levels of religious complexity as it is the search for some new simple orthodoxy, as in the case of a student recently reported to me by a teacher of religion. After three or four lectures on Confucianism this professor was surprised by a young man after class who said, "Scratch one Presbyterian; add one Confucian." What we are talking about is a cultural phenomenon that has been in preparation at least since the early 19th century and will be with us long after the current fads are forgotten. In particular a shallow and easy eclecticism about religion is not at all what I mean by symbolic realism. In order to prevent departments of religion from opting for such an eclecticism a continuing intense dialectic with the first and second forms of consciousness is necessary.

Paul Ricoeur has spoken of a "second naiveté" to characterize the religious consciousness that follows upon rational criticism[4] and I have found in that phrase an apt expression of the religious attitude of the third form of religious consciousness. But surely a second naïveté is only possible if one has taken what must in contrast be called primary naïveté with profound seriousness. To live wholly grasped in one of the great traditional religious symbolisms is not a thing lightly to be dismissed. Only when we begin to penetrate what that might mean, with all the painful difficulty, the hard work with language and history that are necessary for such penetration, are we even in a position to begin to think about "second naïveté." To some extent the third form of religious consciousness requires a degree of experience not often available to the young. It is easy to feign, difficult to achieve. It is true that Robert Lifton in his concept of Protean Man[5] has given us an image of personality among the young which might make this form of religious consciousness readily available, but it remains to be seen how many protean men and women are living in a genuinely multiplex reality and how many are merely avoiding all but the most superficial commitments.

Not only is a deep exposure to primary naïveté necessary for the full development of second naïveté but so is a deep exposure to criticism. Here too the young, with their deep aversion to subjecting anything, certainly anything as delicate as religion, to searching analysis, will have many difficulties and the teacher of religion who caters to such attitudes by presenting only unanalyzed images will not help them. If modern man can be religious again it will be because he has absorbed to the bottom all the achievements of critical scholarship and critical social science, not because he has ignored them. It is necessary for a department of religion to uphold the tradition of critical scholarship and analysis even while recognizing its limitations.

And yet it will probably also be in departments of religion that those limitations will be most forcefully criticized. Plato said that all education is initiation and Whitehead said that all education is religious and yet the ethos of the secular university has singularly ignored that fact. Or rather it has disguised its own initiatory and religious proclivities in the stance of scientific objectivity. At the root of the belief that cognitive rationality is the highest good, the operative value system of the secular university, is a fundamental view of man and the universe for which I am prepared to use the term religious—or perhaps several such views of man. We can discern at least two: one the stance of liberal optimism that the progress of science and the progress of man are identical, that men are basically good and that when reason triumphs over error they will in fact be so; one the stance of realistic pessimism, that human history is a massive abberation and that the life of reason is the only thing in it worth trying to save. There are few places left in the university, and the department of religion is perhaps chief among them, where it is possible to say that cognitive rationality is only one human good among others and that unless it exists in the context of the cultivation of moral, religious and aesthetic sensitivity the consequences may be monstrously destructive. The department of religion may be able to contribute not only the sense of the specificity of its own subject matter and of the high canons of critical scholarship necessary for its analysis but also a sense of education as initiation into the mysteries of existence. If it can even begin to achieve that last goal without slighting its other obligations, it can make an enormous contribution to overcoming the desiccation not only of our universities but of our culture.

Notes

[1] See my article "Christianity and Symbolic Realism," the comments by Samuel Z. Klausner and Benjamin Nelson, and my reply in the *Journal for the Scientific Study of Religion*, 9, 2, Summer 1970, pp. 89-115.

[2] *Beyond Belief*, Harper and Row, 1970, chapter 15, "Between Religion and Social Science."

[3] Mircea Eliade was particularly well trained in Indian religion though he uses the whole range of oriental scholarship with ease. Jung has been a major psychological influence on him but I believe Durkheim has also deeply influenced him, perhaps in ways of which even he is not fully aware. Norman O. Brown is deeply versed in psychoanalysis but also in the whole tradition of Western social thought as well as widely read in oriental religion. He is, of course, also a distinguished classicist. Herbert Fingarette has been influenced by psychoanalysis and particularly by Chinese religion, though also by Indian thought. Paul Ricoeur is deeply conversant with Freud and though not with oriental religion narrowly conceived, I think his close familiarity with the mythology of the ancient near east performs for him an analogous function. Fingarette and Ricoeur are of course both philosophers, though not, I think, typical ones in today's philosophical ambience.

[4] Paul Ricoeur, *The Symbolism of Evil*, Beacon Press, 1969, p. 351.

[5] Robert Jay Lifton, *History and Human Survival*, Random House, 1970, Chapter 15 and passim.

Hot Gospel in a Cool College?
The Question of Advocacy

James Tunstead Burtchaell, C.S.C.

Continual doubt is cast upon the study of religion as appropriate to a serious college or university. The question is put: do religion departments teach their subject academically or do they advocate religion in a partisan sort of way? Is their ultimate aim—covertly or overtly—to elicit from their students a commitment, or to enable them to make a dispassionate assessment? Is wisdom or faith the point of the enterprise? The clear implication in these queries is that if religion be presented in a hortatory, proselytizing fashion by teachers who really wish to encourage belief and devotion in their students, then it ought not be confused with nor ranged among the legitimate disciplines cultivated within the academy. The classroom is not for preaching.

Causes have existed for this inquiry to be made. For one thing, the preponderant majority of teachers who staff departments of religion or theology have been ordained to the ministry, priesthood, or rabbinate. In the case of Catholics, many are members of religious orders. All these men and women have accepted an explicit commission to recruit fellow-believers. Professors not in orders have traditionally been required to undergo the standard course in a theological college, and to obtain the B.D. or equivalent degree as a condition of admission to doctoral studies in religion. Thus even if ministry was no aim of theirs, they were processed through a course of study that was professionally oriented. Still others who teach in the field may have taken all their studies in institutions conducted under the auspices of a single church. Thus nearly all personnel in the field seem to have undertaken or to have been assimilated to an active role as officers of their denominations. They are professional advocates.

There are now 800 colleges and universities in the United States that maintain some sort of religious affiliation, usually through relation to a church. In this context, there has been an institutional concern for advocacy quite distinct from the motivations of the individual faculty members. One of the founding aims of such schools, operative in their religion or theology departments, has been that the faith and church-fidelity of the students be preserved. The study of religion was openly designed for catechetical purposes, to strengthen and support orthodoxy.

A third ground for doubt arises when one considers the issues

---

James T. Burtchaell is Provost, University of Notre Dame.

that have occupied the attention of religion teachers. Sects have for so long identified themselves by their peculiarities, and their proponents have thus laid extraordinary emphasis upon points at issue with other denominations or churches. Much energy and discussion have been sacrificed to bickering. The result is a loss of balance. Lutherans have tended to devote large tracts of their curricula to Reformation studies. Orthodox Jews have studied the customs that have protected them from assimilation by Christian majorities. Catholics have endlessly quoted papal documents. Even when these studies were neither trivial nor truculent (though this they often were), they created an imbalance of concern that discredited the field among scholars at large.

Examinations and grading have ever been a vexation to students. Some serious educators grumble today that they inhibit study more than they motivate it, and various accommodations are here and there tried. Independent of this general discussion, though, there has repeatedly been put forward the view that the case is unique for religious studies: there must be neither testing nor grading because the purpose of the courses transcends mere academic credit or degrees. One is exploring a lifestyle, an overall purpose and commitment. This kind of language understandably makes academics wary, and provides one more reason to suspect that this is no proper discipline for a serious college.

Several years ago Governor Reagan of California appointed a commission, known by the name of Max Rafferty, its chairman, to report on the propriety of introducing the study of religion into state schools. The commission favored the idea, but its understanding of what religious studies are was not overly suasive. It called for publicly sponsored religious studies as the last best hope for the American Way of Life so threatened at present by socialism, communism, and other deviations from traditional, national values. To read the Report is to be reminded at a distance of the cult of blood, class, and country in the Hitler Youth Movement. Now admittedly the commission was mostly considering lower education, and its report has not had much effect in the state. But it speaks for many citizens in the country who think that this is why religion should be taught in universities, and would lend their support only on these terms. One more reason, then, for men of letters, who have so repeatedly had to battle for the freedom and legitimacy of untrammeled study, to discount religion departments as ersatz and alien intrusions in the academy.

The atmosphere among theologians, not surprisingly, tends to be one of retreat. At church-affiliated schools it has long been a tradition that all students, or at least those of the sponsoring denomination, be required to obtain certain credits in religious studies. The trend today is for these course requirements to be radically reduced, or often eliminated altogether. This in turn causes a shrinkage in the size of departmental faculty. There are different symptoms on the campuses of secularized universities: that is, schools originally founded under religious auspices but subsequently transmuted into purely private schools with no operative religious orientation. One notices here that the religion faculty assume a markedly defensive timidity. Their colleagues evidently do not suffer theologians gladly. Thus the latter keep a low profile, and strive at every turn to exhibit Scholarliness. State colleges, as is commonly known, are now moving to create departments of religious studies where none previously existed. Lest one see in this a wave of unqualified welcome, it is sobering to note that in numerous instances there were committees of earnest faculty or legislators opposed to the move, regarding the subject of religion as hardly more qualified for inclusion than Surfing II or Calisthenics 143.

Most of the negative indicators which but recently could have been cited against the subject in universities, are now reversing themselves. For example, most entering scholars in the field are laymen or laywomen, and the current trend in graduate programs is to accept students directly from their first degree without requiring the divinity school course. On church-affiliated campuses the distinction between chaplaincy and theological study has become functionally clear. The ecumenical movement brings more measured tones to theological debate. But even before this, savants had created a common market of religious scholarship wherein Christians, Jews, and Orientals have depended upon and contended with one another with less acrimony, say, than is the custom in philosophical circles, or in the average English department. And the record shows that the course of study for the doctorate in this single field is more painstaking than that in any other. In a word, religious studies need make no excuses.

I would not consider the objections reviewed earlier to constitute reliable evidence today that religion is inappropriate as a field of study in a university or college. Queries continue, though, and two remain to be considered. The first concerns public education alone. Should religion courses and departments be permitted in schools conducted by the state? There is considerable bias against them. The First Amendment to the Constitution, prohibiting the establishment of religion by Congress, is repeatedly invoked to prevent government subsidy for religious enterprises. Admittedly its application has been uneven and inconsistent. This is to be expected, since the church-state tradition has been built, not upon the amendment itself (which forbids only a state church), but upon a judicial opinion that has largely been supported by public sentiment, if not by the Constitution itself. Similar and more specific prohibitions have been written into many constitutions of the several states through various forms of the Blaine Amendment. The point, though, exceeds strict law. American public policy has been hostile toward affording the shelter of public institutions or the support of public monies to any enterprise which would propagate religion. By extension, this same policy is asked to cast an unwelcoming shadow over even the study of religion. The campaign against state involvement in religion waged by the American Civil Liberties Union and the American Jewish Congress has not explicitly raised this issue, but has generally moved in a direction and sustained the kind of argument that would not be favorable.

Religion departments in state universities have been correspondingly cautious. One finds in their catalogues, for example, courses on "The Bible as Literature." Often this is a purely diversionary rubric for a serious course in scripture study. But why does one never see courses in other departments on "Seneca as Literature," or "Das Kapital as Literature," or "Clausewitz as Literature?" Why is suspicion of advocacy reserved for religious studies?

This really raises a broader issue, one that I have not seen receive much attention. There are numerous activities which have been considered appropriate within universities, yet become problematic if the university is an agency of the state. It has been a constant conviction in America that government must be constitutionally inhibited from interfering in some matters where it might be tempted to meddle or to oppress. The founding fathers were anxious about the possible re-assertion of absolutism, and explicitly declared certain issues out of bounds for the state. Their wariness of government and officials wanes in our day, but it is still there. Does this inhibition upon the state mesh well with the freedom of a university? George Bernard Shaw once snorted that a Catholic university was a contradiction in terms: meaning, one supposes, that the church could not tolerate completely untrammeled inquiry. But how about the state? Should a public college be subjected to the same curbs which we impose upon the state itself? Professor Rostow, for instance, enjoys a freedom at the University of Texas to make political comments that might be inappropriate were he a civil servant of the State of Texas. But is he not? The Supreme Court, in overturning the Connecticut statute banning contraceptives, affirmed that the government had no business invading the privacy of the marriage bed. What then of the sexual research conducted lo! these many years by Alfred Kinsey's institute at the University of Indiana?

Briefly: does the freedom of the university perhaps require, or at least make it preferable, that it not be an agency administered by government, but rather a private institution for the public welfare, governed independently even though subsidized by the state? Would we not do well to distinguish direct support from public aegis, thus freeing the schools clearly from those inhibitions we have so constantly hung upon our governments? And if so, would this not alleviate any reasonable concern about the study of religion under state auspices?

But let us go further, to consider the single most powerful bias against religious studies in all colleges: state, private, and church-affiliated. There is, and for some years has been, a single model of scholarship dominant in higher education. It was first developed by the physical sciences, then was adopted by the social sciences, and has of late appeared widely in the humanities. I refer to the model of empirical, scientific verification. The methodology is now old and mature in disciplines such as physics. It is still vigorously new in fields like philosophy (linguistic analysis, for instance), psychology (behaviorism), and literature (certain schools of criticism). It was a method ruthlessly opposed at first by scholastic philosophers and divines, but it has gained the honors of the academy and has enormously enhanced learning.

It may not be immune, though, to that very intolerance from which it suffered in its own early days. Many practitioners of the scientific method who know no other forms of scholarly inquiry or discourse are drawn to regard these other activities as matters of guesswork, whim, or emotion. This begets a snootiness that easily turns upon theology. The scientific method is not unknown in the field. In biblical studies particularly there have been scholars unready to countenance any inquiry that might move beyond literary analysis into doctrinal speculation. But for the most part, the field of religious studies has developed a variety of methodologies that are a mystery to academics versed only in the dominant method. And to them they have the smack of pure advocacy.

One outcome of this scientific disdain—for the humanities as well as for divinity—is a readiness by scholars to venture into authoritative pronouncements touching other disciplines. Thus the nation hears nuclear physicists giving testimony on foreign policy, surgeons elaborating their positions on ethics, and astronomers paid to lecture on philosophy. Now I am far from suggesting that theologians should ally themselves with colleagues in the humanities to fend off the well-meaning but untutored scientists. Nor is this an illustration of Belloc's quip that politics and religion are the subjects any fool will speak of in a pub. Instead, I would observe there is a very significant asymmetry between these diverse areas of understanding.

There is no necessity for any man to be initiated into the scholarship of science, mathematics, or technology. It is desirable and illuminating, enjoyable and profitable. But it is not needful. For the society, perhaps, but never for any individual. By contrast, all men have a common stake in the humanities and in divinity. The fact that physicists discourse on politics is no matter for grudge among political scientists and historians. It simply shows that every citizen *will* have convictions on politics. He cannot be prevented, nor should he be. But woe to him and to the nation if he brings to politics only his training as a physicist.

A full and rich education may give a man access to theoretical physics, isotopic biochemistry, environmental engineering, or geophysics. Better for him, better for society that he learn these things. But the study of poetry, history, religion, politics, ethics, mythology—this is not optional in the same sense. These touch on matters that every man speculates upon, and scholarly initiation is needed so that a man may gain sophistication in listening critically and opining cautiously.

Much of the disdain and suspicion directed by masters of the scientific method against scholars of religion testifies more to the narrowness of the former than of the latter. Men acquainted with but a single procedure of understanding must inevitably imagine that the work in religious studies is little more than unexamined prejudice. If colleges and universities continue to award degrees to men upon whom they have conferred proficiency in science or technology, while denying them a liberal education in the humane studies and in religion, then this unlettered carping against theology will never be abated.

Now, to speak directly to the issue of advocacy, I would argue that there should be plenty of it in the college classroom, and that it need make no apology. Somehow neutrality has been assumed to be a guarantee of objective scholarship. Not so. The difference between an ideologue who abuses the academic privilege, and a legitimate teacher, is this: the latter, albeit resolutely committed to certain beliefs, values, policies, initiates his students in the documents and skills wherewith to evaluate the convictions of their teacher, themselves, and others. Bad advocacy refuses to examine its own presuppositions; it ignores the points at dispute. Sincere research manages to combine unabashed preferences and advocated positions with self-criticism.

It is often insinuated that unless the teacher be value-free, he will impair the objectivity of his research and unduly impose upon his students. But no one is value-free. No one could be. Indeed, no one should be if he is to preside over the wonder and inquiry of young minds.

The academy is remote from the practical order. This is the price it willingly pays for freedom. It is a house of words, where one allows no stay or check upon what he reads, hears, or says. But the word is powerful, and the most recondite scholarship erupts into activity. Probably more political revolt has been spawned in the reading room of the British Museum than anywhere else in the world.

Any professor of religion will be handling the tinder, kindling, and fuel of commitment. With the sparks that most young people strike around them, there is going to be a blaze. This is well, provided only that the professor be constantly provoking his younger colleagues to query in a rigorous and responsible way their own convictions.

Education without advocacy is impossible in some disciplines.

Consider, for example, a department of drama where students were coached in the arts of performance, but denied any discernment or judgment about the pieces they were to present, no awareness that Plautus and Jonson and Ionesco had left to their care most potent and persuasive dramas that claim to embody the truth. If the drama teacher and student care not to evaluate and to take stands regarding the truthfulness of what they play, they may be craftsmen, but never educated; *pagliacci,* but never men. The study of drama could degenerate into debating: the ability to pursue a point, careless of its worth. And schools would produce . . . the sort of actors we have upon the stage today.

Theology comes under sharpest criticism from the direction of the social sciences, where strongest claim is made for objectivity, in the belief that whoever advocates anything which cannot be subjected to empirical scrutiny, must be irresponsible. Theologians do tend to be bashful before this accusation, but they should be vexed instead, for many who make the charge are themselves both unwilling and incapable of assessing the considerable corpus of dogma from which they themselves operate.

In many ways the study of religion has singular claims to respect in the university. It possesses and studies the most ancient body of documentation. Its inquiries into hermeneutics and history are the oldest in the world of learning. Its subject matter manifests concerns and experiences more international and transcultural than any other. And it has adhesions with other fields of study that make it perhaps the most interdisciplinary in higher education.

One further point. Scholars in this field are as aware as any of the gnostic nonsense that faith can lead men to. Precisely because they are scrutiners of faith they are more able to query their own presuppositions and bring them to account. The religious scholar may have more perspective than most, for he remembers well so many heady movements that felt they had the world by the tail, and heaven too.

Religion as an Academic Discipline

Peter Slater

In this essay, I want to consider the problem of integrity in a program of religious studies. For many of us, the initial identity crises are over. Our departments are a recognized feature of the academic landscape. We have proved our independence of our mother churches. We have demonstrated that we are an inter-departmentalist's dream by forging alliances with Philosophy, History, English, Art, Music, Classics, Sociology, Psychology and Asian Studies. We have played the numbers game and won, so that enrollments in our courses are a talking-point when it comes to the annual fight for new appointments. We are respectable in the secular world. But in the process we have come close to losing our souls. Our courses are so cluttered with Camus and Cleaver, Marcuse and Norman Brown, that we would be hard pressed to guess what department's selections we were looking at, were we to see our required readings stacked up along the bookstore walls. We are typical adolescents—self-assertive yet unsure of ourselves, obsessed with how we look to our peers, growing in the power to be ourselves, but *without discipline*. No wonder the Sophomores love us! It is time that we came of age.

For most of us, the parental discipline against which we have been rebelling is that of theology. Given a solid grounding in biblical studies and dogmatic history ourselves, with only an occasional apologetic tilt at psychology and other religions, we have awakened from our sectarian slumbers to discover a fascinating land of myth and folklore outside the seminary walls. And we have realized how much of what we learned within comes under the same headings of myth and folklore. We have looked at what every minister knows—that life in the parish is not as his professors had described it—and recognized as religion the vast range of rituals and commitments that was not comprehended in our theology. If we were Barthians, we proclaimed that Christ had come to save us from all this. If we were Tillichians, we found points of correlation between the Christ of German Classical Idealism and the culture of the suburbs. In any case, we were absorbing the strange new world of Modern Man, for whom the quarrels of Chalcedon were hardly news, let alone Good News.

The big shift has been in the direction of social studies. We have discovered "civil religion in America."[1] We have discerned

Peter Slater is Associate Professor of Religion, Carleton University, Ottawa, Canada. This essay was published in an abbreviated form in the Bulletin of the Council on the Study of Religion (II/4, October 1971) and is used by permission.

the priestly roles of politicians, psychiatrists, PR men and news-paper pundits. We have thrilled at the thought that the propagand-ists of the New Left may be the prophets of our time. We have grown gray watching Bergmann's projections of bourgeois boredom into the Middle Ages. Whereas our fathers wrestled with "an-swers" to the latest philosophical professions of atheism, we have learned to look through such intellectualized ghosts of by-gone arguments at the host of gods and goblins populating our comic books, our automobile advertisements and such cultural pap as Playboy Magazine. But so far, our looking has tended to have no more system to it than that of an annual stocktaking. We have classified what's on the shelves in the manner of an American van der Leeuw.[2] But now that we have gathered all that data, what are we to do with it?

The pioneers in our departments were mostly brought up on the principle of "data for data's sake." They were so afraid of ex-hibiting any kind of theological commitment—or so fed up with the heresy hunts of theologians—that they simply laid out one world religion after another before the awestruck students, with-out any suggestion of right or wrong beliefs. Just to pronounce all those Sanskrit and Chinese names correctly was enough of an achievement, without venturing onto the shaky ground of norma-tive judgments. Inevitably, the students chose up sides, being either fascinated with things foreign or reconfirmed in their prior convictions. But they were not taught any principles of criticism to guide them in their choices. Even today we fail to teach our stu-dents the art of assessing commitments as an academic exercise, though most of us believe that a man without commitments is only half a man.

Without belittling the achievements of our predecessors or sliding back into the parochialism of the seminaries, we need now to develop some sense of the principles and purposes governing the study of religion in universities and colleges, if we are to inte-grate our data into the liberal arts curriculum. The rest of this es-say is meant to open discussion of this issue. I focus on the concept of an undergraduate major in religion as the point at which our problems become most obvious and acute.

All too often religion at the undergraduate level continues to represent a conglomerate of interests rather than an initiation into critical thinking on a given subject. If our seniors have gained some sense of discipline, it has generally come from their cognate courses in related fields. Otherwise, they have become alive to questions, perhaps, but hardly equipped to sort out the possible answers in any methodical way. They have not been given enough mastery of the subject to mold a lifetime of reflection and further reading. In an important sense, their intellects have remained untrained so that, while they have tended to be less hidebound than their peers, they have gone on thinking about things after graduation as political scientists, philosophers or psychologists, rather than as students of religion.

We could rationalize the current situation on many of our campuses by arguing that the concept of an academic discipline is obsolete. It is true that subjects which once only co-existed uneasily are now breaking down barriers and finding new points of contact (for instance, ethics and psychology). But behind labels such as "discipline" and "field" is the more important matter of the difference between a trained intellect and an untrained one. Out of this arises the questions of what it means to say that one has concentrated on the study of religion and whether such a study constitutes a discipline in its own right.

Of course, some kinds of discipline are acquired irrespective of subject matter, such as how to read a book, how to write a term-paper and how to uncover gratuitous assumptions of one kind or another. Also, it is true that, by virtue of seminars on such major figures as Aquinas and Schleiermacher, our students "catch" some sense of subject and method from the works of these men. We teach more than we suppose, even though it isn't always "Religion!" But just as, in faculty meetings, we may enjoy the spectacle of trained minds mulling over major (and minor!) issues—now the economist's, now the chemist's, now the linguist's—so I should like to add to our society, for the sake of its mental and moral health and the enrichment of our culture, men and women whose training has been to think things through self-consciously as students of Religion. We have in hand the makings of an exciting new subject with a "logic" and set of interests of its own.

What, then, is religion and the study of religion? We could spend all day on each part of this question, but we won't. As Wittgenstein has taught us, definitions are not to be mistaken for blueprints.[3] They set the parameters of our investigations for us, not the precise meaning for every possible use of our terms. Tillich's rough definition is as useful a beginning as any: religion is that which concerns me ultimately (das mich unbedingt angeht).[4] It allows for the social scientist's recognition that what actually concerns me isn't always what I admit to being concerned with and the existentialist's insistence on the "for me" element in religion. Some have said that the definition is too little receptive to the idea that religion is what God demands of us and too enamored of the idea that it is merely the projection of my dreams and nightmares. But they have missed the connotations of the original German.[5] The definition cannot be read undialectically, either in the direction of pure subjectivity or its opposite. We may point to its systematic ambiguities and vague bridging of possibly impassable chasms, but not to its excessive emphasis on the isolated ego. Tillich was too big a man to be purely egotistical, either in life or in thought.

What is lacking in Tillich's shorthand definition is some re-cognition of the social shape that our concerns have taken in the past and of the place that we give to our lessor concerns in the light of our ultimate concern. We have not studied Buddhism, for instance, if we give attention solely to Satori as introduced in Suzuki's more popular writings. We have to consider also the role of "Dana" (gift-giving) in the lives of the laymen and the presence of the Sangha in the community at large.[6] Likewise, we have not studied Brahmanism if we confine our researches to the last of the four "goals" in life and leave out sex and politics. (One look at the temple walls in India is enough to discredit any such omission!) There is good reason for including the Arabian Nights with the Qur'an in a study of Islam, Graham Greene as well as a Missal when contrasting Gnosticism with Catholicism. We need to con-sider not only the peak experiences in the history of religions but also the ways in which interpretations of these have percolated down to affect the conduct of daily life. We need to acknowledge where religion shades into other affairs as well as what brings them all into focus.

What Tillich's definition does do for us, however, is to set our eyes firmly on the fact that, whatever else, religion brings up the question of priorities. A religious life is one conditioned by a sense of certain priorities and the study of religion is, accord-ingly, a study of these priorities. We may gather what these priori-ties are, and so obtain some idea of what subjects should be en-countered in courses on religion, if we elaborate somewhat on Tillich's definition. I offer the following: *a religion is a personal way of life informed by traditional elements of creed, code and cult and directed towards the realization of some transcendent end-state* (e.g. Nirvana or Olympian bliss).

It is the reference to transcendence that makes of religion more than a recollection of past glories. Appeal to our ultimate end is what gives the prophet his principle of criticism against the priestly tradition. The realization of such an end is discerned in the lives of saints, incarnations of deities and founders of communities, whose stories are told on high holy days. Appeal to the traditions celebrating their achievements is what gives the priest his authority in asserting the power of some ways over others as the approved ones for realizing our goals. Ancient myths, sagas and legends are the stuff of religion not only because of the ideas that they convey but also, and more importantly, because of the examples that they provide and the attitudes and intentions that they communicate. I can share the attitudes and intentions of Isaiah, for instance, long after men have ceased thinking in terms of cherubim in the holy of holies. From my nurture in his tradition, I come to appreciate what concerned him ultimately and so to express this same ultimate concern in my own day and age. It is the transcendent end, given highest priority within a tradition, that provides us with some persepctive on the everyday problems of ordinary existence. By studying a number of traditions, therefore, we become aware of a variety of possible ends and their consequences for our conduct. We become critically aware of what the real or imagined options are—natural, supernatural, immanent, transcendent and so forth.

By "personal way of life" I mean both individual and communal ways. In this connection, it is noteworthy that most of us are adherents of more than one religion or quasi-religion. It is a rare man whose commitments constitute a consistent set and whose practice matches his promises. Many a lapsed son of Israel, for instance, still celebrates his son's Bar Mitzvah and many an erstwhile Catholic or Protestant gets married in a church. We are more like the Orientals than we care to admit, going to one tradition for weddings, another for funerals and still another for our moral codes. If we take religion out of Sunday School and see it as the priority dimension of our culture, then we shall see clearly how the cult of the State still conflicts with faith in Yahweh, the quest for fertility still militates against monogamy and the dream of lasting happiness still yokes world-denying and world-affirming tendencies in unlikely combinations. It is a disciplined spirit indeed that subdues all yearnings for utopia, all symptoms of hero-worship and all inclinations to hedge one's bets by worshipping at the altar of more than one "god." Now that we have taken off our sectarian spectacles, we are beginning to see "religion" again in all its forms and sacred places, in "the hunt" at work as well as in the bridal chamber at home. And we are beginning to appreciate the relevance of the study of religion to the conduct of life in the twentieth century.

It follows from what I have said that the study of religion includes not only the history of the formation of various creeds, but also the comparative study of codes and cults. It encompasses the "high" traditions of the major world religions and the "low" traditions of the less sophisticated. The scholar in religion grasps how a Gandhi could attack untouchability from within and an Augustine could feel the fall of Rome to be a religious crisis. He may not be religious himself, in any traditional sense, but he knows how to distinguish the true from the false amongst priests and prophets, even as he shares in a culture that leans rather on columnists and professors. He appreciates the contexts in which they came to their decisions and made their compromises. And he masters the principles whereby they distinguished between hypocrisy and good politics. He knows that there are rationalizations as well as reasons in religion and takes account of "non-theological" as well as of theological factors undergirding the religious life. He uses all the aids to investigation available to man in the secular world while appreciating that secularity is not the whole story. It is this scholar whose intellectual heirs we have to train.

If, now, we look at college programs in religion with these definitions and observations in mind, we may see why much of the material that is there belongs there and how we may bring some discipline into our discussions of the data. Obviously, many students still need to be given an expanded consciousness of the religious phenomena in our culture. They must become sensitive to the religious dimensions of life exemplified in "secular" literature as well as in scripture, alert to the paganism of today as well as of yesterday. They must acquire the vocabulary of myth and ritual, sacred and profane, church and sect, exegesis and eschatology. They must appreciate both the anti-religious intent of men like Nietzsche, Marx and Freud and the religious themes of alienation and reconciliation which permeate their works. They must see ways of life for what they are — wholes made out of jumbles of hopes, fears, ideals and prejudices that determine our rational-irrational responses to our environment. To initiate them into this kind of awareness is, I think, the task of a good introductory course.[7]

But it is not much use talking to students about the "paganism" of today if they have no knowledge of the major forms of religious experience and expression in the past. They must learn to put their own tacit traditions in their historical contexts, seeing the Bible against the background of the Ancient Near East, setting Christian theology in the milieu of Hellenistic culture. In this connection, I maintain that every major in religion should know some set of scriptures — the Bible, the Qur'an, the Veda, the Tripitaka or the Confucian Canon — and the history of its interpretation. He should know why these and not other writings were chosen for their communities and what it means to reflect systematically on their contents. He must know what priorities dictate the choice of proof-texts in a tradition and how to argue by appeal to the tradition for conclusions other than those of the orthodox. Unless he is engaged in a program of interdisciplinary studies he should, ideally, gain some sense of the original languages and know more than one set of scriptures or stream of oral tradition. He need not become a fundamentalist or get bogged down in the factional squabbles of best-forgotten Europeans, but he should know how to reason on the basis of various kinds of revelation and have some control of the historical data that, in religion, restrain our speculative impulses. He must know why "pure" reason has not always been given highest priority in the deliberations of men. In short, he must learn to respect authority — when it is appropriate to do so.

We have by now mentioned more than enough material to provide the meat for our intermediary courses. Most of us include these subjects at the upper levels, if we have not instead offered several opening courses in which introductory and historical materials are interspersed.[8] This latter alternative, incidentally, has the advantage of giving the students surveys of the various sub-fields of religion, such as world religions and religion and society, whereas the single introduction brings them to the upper-level courses equipped with a common set of concepts, in terms of which to discuss new material. But what concerns me now is the sense of purpose and accomplishment with which we leave our seniors, whichever sequence they have followed through to their final year.

A graduate in religion should be one who can systematically tease out our hidden allegiances by comparing various ways of life with each other—ways in which similar values are weighted differently and conflicting goals are given highest priority. Where the philosopher is trained to detect presuppositions concerning the nature of being and the manner of knowing, the student of religion should ask after the meanings given to life by the values which we prize the most. He need not be a theologian but should rather appreciate critically the consistencies and inconsistencies within *whatever* tradition a man stands. He should be like the philosopher in depending upon data supplied by others and like the historian in poring over the actual decisions of individuals and communities. But he should have his own distinctive training and sense of discipline, gained not from any single course required in his last semester but from the way in which all his classes in religion have been conducted from beginning to end.[9]

Personally, I believe that the end for which we all strive in religion is some kind of freedom. The study of religion is for me the study of man's quest to be free, in and of himself, from and for the world. Of course, the ways to freedom are as various as our conceptions of it, including complete alienation from things physical and utter absorption in mundane matters. We may think of freedom in primarily political terms, primarily personal terms or as some composite of these. We may believe that we must kill God in order to be free or that we can only be free by His grace. The religions of the world exemplify the options exercised by mankind and point up the consequences of giving one kind of freedom priority over another. For instance, Manicheeism entails the repudiation of compromise and exaltation of the life of the "spirit." As such, it is anti-political. By contrast, Marxism is equally against compromise but is thoroughly political.[10] Not all ways to freedom are religious, since some conceptions of it are thoroughly immanentist. But as various ways are shaped by a proleptic or realized eschatology which is more or less utopian they fall clearly into the category of the religious. Here again we must recall that religious ways of life shade off into non-religious ways of life as our ultimate concern blends in with our intermediate concerns.

Some colleagues from other departments have complained that I cast our net too widely and ought to focus more systematically on problems concerning God and man. The quest for freedom is for them a problem for the social sciences. In fact, I regard God as the one who makes true freedom possible and prefer the religions of grace to the elitist efforts of the yogis. But I regard the separation between religion and politics or theology and history as a relatively modern development, which distorts by its divisions at least as much as it fosters fruitful specialization. I come to talk of freedom from the context of studying and teaching Hinduism, i.e., a set of traditions in which ultimate liberation is given priority over political power in the ascending scale of human aspirations. Besides, there is no conflict, inasmuch as the social scientist studies primarily the instruments whereby men attain to freedom, while the humanist is mainly concerned with concepts of what freedom *should* be for us. In particular, students of religion are concerned with what imperatives follow from particular concepts of freedom, including the freedom of Job's God and John's Gospel.

What gives integrity to our religion is, in any case, not its restriction to a limited segment of our culture but the disciplining of our involvement in the whole of our culture by reference to the ideal end espoused in our tradition. Likewise, what gives integrity to the study of religion is not attention to a limited set of "objects" or cultural artifacts but recognition of the coloring of the whole range of our commitments by a particular quest for freedom. The logic of our priorities is dictated by this quest and our critical insights came from asking whether the tacit or explicit creeds, codes and cults clustered about a particular quest are aids to freedom or instruments of evasion. Judgment comes from both within and without a particular tradition as a result of our outrage at all attempts to keep man in chains (including some that masquerade under the banner of true religion). In this context, we may note that, while we cannot and should not attempt to make our students' commitments for them, we should teach them to recognize commitments that have been made and to deal with them in their own terms.

At this point, some critics still wonder whether the propagandistic itch of those in religion can really be contained in the classroom. In fact, it is an irony of the times that philosophers and historians tend to preach at will to their students, while religion professors are supposed to remain scrupulously noncommittal. I find that it helps my students to become independent of my thinking if I let them know where I stand, after first introducing them to the historical and contemporary alternatives. Furthermore, high among the priorities in the religious life, and implicit in the idea of freedom, is a commitment to Truth. (It is one of the "names" of God).[11] In the history of obscuratism, even among theologians, it is more a man's personal philosophy and conservative class-consciousness than anything deriving from religion as such that accounts for his opposition to new possibilities in his time.[12] The average teacher of religion is, I suspect, no more propagandistically inclined than his colleagues and much more aware than they of risks inherent in giving way to his inclinations.

To repeat, a major in religion should, on my view, be one who has mastered the many traditions and is prepared to make his own way to freedom. He is ready to throw away the crutches of teachers and set syllabi when he knows how to render a religious judgment on any situation or argument in fiction or in daily life. In Wittgenstein's sense, he knows how to "go on" using such central concepts as alienation and freedom, sin and salvation, by extrapolating and applying them to novel conditions. He can discern the sense of identity conveyed by modern myths and distinguish between the authentic and inauthentic rituals that regulate the social traffic of our times. He can appraise not only the theoretical intricacies of our value-judgments, as would a moral philosopher, but also the practical impediments to the ends in view. He is alive to obstructive and constructive resorts to tradition. He can contribute to new creeds in the making and cross-examine old codes in the light of modern concepts of human nature. He resists claims to ultimacy made for any discipline, including his own, because he recognizes the relativity of our achievements in view of our transcendent ends. Throughout, his mind is not tied to any single doctrine of God or dream of life after death. Rather he knows what would count as a Gnostic, a Catholic, a bhankti or karma yoga way of living under new conditions. He *knows* and is ready to make an informed choice for himself, even if he does not choose to follow any tradition personally. And that is all that we should expect from the product of an academy that does not promise salvation to its graduates. As we all know, to be educated in religion is not necessarily to be religious.

How, then, are we to turn this dream student into a reality? I have asserted that no single course will do the job. Neither will the demand for a senior thesis. No one component of the undergraduate program is sufficient. What has to be insisted upon, rather, is some meaningful sequence of courses and requirements which develops a cumulative impulse in the desired direction. Instead of a series of courses which serve as equally good entry-points into the field, we need to stipulate prerequisites for our upper-level courses which spare us from having to explain, ever anew, what is religion, what is a myth and what is the role of tradition. Whether a student concentrates upon biblical studies, non-western studies, social studies or contemporary thought, he must develop the sense of subject, linguistic skills and control of data that mark the scholar off from the pedant. He must come to his senior seminars ready to undertake truly demanding examinations of religious life and thought, or find himself refused admission.

Obviously, in three or four years, a student cannot be expected to become familiar with every feature of religion. I consider it sufficient if he has followed any two sub-fields through the intermediate steps to the advanced seminars—or any one, taken in conjunction with a minor in another subject. In my opinion, he deserves his degree when he realizes how much he doesn't know yet knows where to look for the information that he is lacking and what to ask those who do know. Given an overview of the whole subject, intensive training in some facets of it and time to practice his skills in his senior year, he comes out as much more than just a carbon copy of ourselves. For he evolves from a whole new era in the study of religion.

At a time when we are being overwhelmed with information and inundated with people who experience only what they feel at their finger-tips, we sorely need scholars who can articulate our principles of selection and school us in the making of informed choices concerning our ways of life. Since there is no way of mass-producing such scholars or checking their proficiency mechanically, our only hope is to develop programs which stimulate rather than stultify their minds and to maintain standards by having oral, as well as written, final examinations, in which the incompetent and ill-prepared individual is turned back, while the imaginative and industrious are rewarded. I know that the concept of senior comprehensive exams has been attacked by some students, but I believe that, properly managed, they can prove to be a valuable experience for both examiners and examinees. We can expect to learn much from those who are well-prepared, both before and after graduation, and we have only ourselves to blame if we fail to take the chance.

Finally, it is worth noting that, although we have been considering undergraduate majors who are completing a traditional four-year program, the values inherent in the study of religion are not restricted to this group. In addition to the major in another subject, who picks up religion as his "minor" of part of his distribution requirement, we have to remember the student in the two-year college and the graduate in middle age who returns to take courses for interest not necessarily for credit. If professional schools begin admitting students before their B.A., we may expect this last group to provide us with some of our most challenging students. As adult and continuing education receive professional rather than part-time attention we may see in our classes more and more mature citizens. Already professionally qualified they are beginning to demand courses on meaning and value in modern life of a calibre to compete with the level of expertise that they are accustomed to elsewhere. For such people, the traditional pattern of the liberal arts B.A. may be becoming somewhat obsolete. But the need for the liberalizing arts as part of a comprehensive educational plan has never been greater. Amongst these arts, religion today has earned its place on its merits.

[1]The allusion is to the well-known article by Robert Bellah, reprinted in Lessa and Vogt's Reader in Comparative Religion, second edition.

[2]G. van der Leeuw, Religion in Essence and Manifestations., two volumes, trans. J. C. Turner, ed. H. Penner, Harper Torchbooks, N.Y., 1963.

[3]In Philosophical Investigations, passim.

[4]See Systematic Theology, II, p. 86, et al.

[5]By no stretch of the imagination could someone with Tillich's upbringing be supposed to have regarded 'unbedingt' as a sign of sheer subjectivity. His final allegiance was to Hegel, not to Kierkegaard.

[6]See the article by Richard Robinson in Encyclopedia of World Religions, ed. R. C. Zaehner, and Winston L. King's In the Hope of Nibbana.

[7]For more on this subject, see my short note on "An Introductory Religion Course," Bulletin of the American Academy of Religion, Vol. 35, No. 1, Spring, 1967, pp. 20-2.

[8]The latter is the form followed at Sir George Williams University. It seems to be the more viable for large departments, since it allows each of us to teach his own specialty almost exclusively. As long as our reputations depend in part upon publication and jobs are apportioned on the zoological principle (one of each species), the pressure will be on for this kind of specialization. Graduates from Sir George have gone on especially in the history of religions. From Haverford College, they went into Law, Medicine, Journalism, Architecture, Cinematography, Education and various Ph.D. programs—in fact, anything for which a B.A. might or might not be considered a prerequisite.

[9]At Haverford, the most successful senior seminar was one in which each student was sent to scour the current journals in Religion for an article which he wanted us all to read and discuss. It was here, incidentally, that the discrepancy between our own training in theology and our students' lack of it became apparent.

[10]On Manicheeism in politics, see the paper by William F. May reprinted in Witness to a Generation, ed. Wayne Cowan, Bobbs Merrill, pb.

[11]As an example of this commitment and its possible consequences see Charles Davis, A Question of Conscience, London, 1967.

[12]See J. Dillenberger, Protestant Theology and Natural Science, Doubleday, N.Y. 1963.

The Catholic University and the Academic Study of Religion

William J. Sullivan, S.J.

1. Context

The first task of this essay is to define the context in which the discussion of the academic study of religion in the Catholic university[1] should be carried on. The context for the discussion of the academic study of religion differs radically when one is speaking about a public institution or a private, non-sectarian school on the one hand or about the Catholic university or college on the other. It differs, though perhaps less radically, when one is speaking of the Protestant, church-related college and the Catholic institution. Because of these differences, I do not intend to comment on or to develop the general topic of "the academic study of religion in the American college or university." This is an important topic. It is a topic that is the object of a large body of literature.[2] But the general questions about the academic study of religion are frequently not the specific and concrete questions which confront the Catholic college or university. And to that extent, those general questions are not the correct context nor the appropriate object of these reflections. I am not ignoring the fact that there are voices in this field which are arguing for or predicting a "homogenization" of the study of religion.[3] It is my judgment that such a position overlooks important elements or factors, some of which I will be specifying through the rest of this paper.

Educational administrators and teachers in the area of Religious Studies are conscious of the very considerable development in American higher education over the past two or three decades in the academic study of religion. In effect this has meant the introduction of many programs or departments of religious studies and some schools of religion. This development has led to the search for a rationale which would explain or justify the introduction of such programs. The development of such a rationale was imperative both because these courses or programs were new and because of widespread opposition to them. The literature of religious studies since the Second World War, where it is not simply descriptive, is primarily concerned with this question of a rationale. A primary example of such an attempt is the so-called "Holbrook

William J. Sullivan is Dean of the School of Divinity, St. Louis University. This essay has been published in a slightly different version in the College Newsletter of the College and University Department, National Catholic Educational Association _(4 June 1971) and in the_ Bulletin of the Council on the Study of Religion _(II/5 December 1971) and is used by permission._

thesis" which argues for religion as an area of humanistic studies.[4] But the focal point of the discussion has been the introduction of religious studies into public and private, nonsectarian institutions.

The Catholic college or university finds itself in a very different situation. This is not to say a less difficult situation, but a different one. And it is for that reason that a different and distinctive question about the academic study of religion arises for the Catholic School. In the case of the Catholic institution, the question is not the reasons for the introduction of courses on religion but the articulation of a rationale for the existing programs in theology and the reformation of the programs according to a consistent and coherent rationale. Thus for the Catholic institution the emphasis is not on reasons for introducing programs but on the effective coordination of such programs with the ideals of the institution expressed academically. This is a different problem, a different context, and therefore a different type of rationale is needed.

Catholic colleges and universities have a history of the teaching of theology in various forms. The schools, departments or programs in this area are established and accepted. But—and this is where the need of a new rationale manifests itself—most of these programs and courses were originally established for a purpose which is no longer functional. These programs were originally established for an apologetic or "custodial" purpose. Their goal was to maintain the young Catholic in his faith, to arm him against various attacks upon his religious belief. Such a goal is no longer a realistic nor an effective one. It is no longer the working goal of most of those who are teaching in this field. Hence there has been felt among administrators and teachers in Catholic institutions a parallel but very different need to articulate a rationale for programs in theology or religious studies in the Catholic college or university. An example of such an effort is the "New Rationale" developed by the 1969 Denver Workshop of the Jesuit Educational Association.[5]

I would take the development of such a rationale to be one of the primary tasks for those concerned with education in Catholic institutions in the 1970's. The first point which I have tried to make is that the context for this discussion is significantly different for the Catholic educator and that the rationale for the program must be developed out of this context. The simple importation of other rationales will not do. I would like to go on now to discuss three elements of that context which would substantially affect the working out of a rationale.

2. Relation

A first task in the discussion of the academic study of religion in the Catholic institution is the clarification of the relation between the work of the department of theology or religious studies and that of other religion-related groups.

The basis of this clarification is the fundamental question of the difference between theology and religion. I am using the term "theology" here in a very wide sense to denote the study of, the reflection on, the systematic construction of, and the communication of the sources, insights, and expressions of religious activity. "Religion" I use to mean the activity itself, that is, the level of action, of experience, of praxis. Liturgy is religion, not theology; so is prayer. Biblical source criticism and method of correlation and hermeneutics are theology, not religion.

Before one can speak at all of the *academic* study of religion, it seems clear to me that some such distinction must be made and accepted. There is a difference between religion and theology, just as there is between poetry and poetics, between painting and art appreciation, between literary creativity and literary criticism. This is not to say that the two realities in any of these cases are not related; they are clearly. But they are distinct types of activities and nothing is to be gained by confusing them.

The purpose of theology is knowledge; it is for this reason that it can be discussed as an academic study. Its direct, immediate "product" is not conduct. This is the object of religion, i.e., a certain form of conduct. Certainly, theology or religious studies as this is understood in the Catholic tradition is related to conduct, but in a mediated fashion; and that mediation is provided by knowledge.

This distinction and relation can be exemplified by considering the relation between theology and religious education. This is a very important distinction, important that is, if theology or religious studies is to have its definition or identity as an academic study. Theology is not religious education, and vice versa. Religious education is life education. It is oriented directly toward praxis; a great deal of religious education is practice, in the literal sense of the term. It consists of introductions into the life of the religious community, into its rites, its symbols, and into its set of moral values. Theology, on the other hand, is focused primarily on understanding. Its immediate object is not the *practicum* but the *intellectum*. It is knowledge, a very special kind of knowledge that has an intrinsic relation to life because it is value-knowledge; but it still remains in the realm of knowledge.

Nothing is gained by confusing religious education and theology. And when it comes to the life of the college or university, to its work of research and teaching, something very important can be lost by not making and observing some such distinction. And what is lost is the vital work of the reflection, the construction, and the communication of the *intellectum* of the Christian faith.

I would suggest that the clarification of this distinction is of particular importance for the Catholic institution of higher education, and this for several reasons. One is the "custodial" context in which the religion or theology department arose in most Catholic schools. There is an element of history, of past practice here, which influences a religious education approach. Another reason is that the persons particularly interested in and responsible for the religious life of the students, i.e., priests and nuns, are frequently also doing the teaching in the theology area. For these and other reasons, this distinction has not been made consistently and effectively in Catholic colleges. But if there is to be an academic program, an academic study of religion, it is the first distinction which must be made and observed.

It may be that a given school at the college level will choose to offer a program of religious education rather than one in theology. Examples of this can certainly be found, particularly in smaller institutions. The merits of such a decision or orientation must be discussed in terms of the situation of the students of this particular institution, their educational needs, etc. But what must be clearly asserted is that such a program should not be called theology or religious studies. Such a religious education orientation takes the program completely out of the area of the academic study of religion.

3. Tradition

Another specific feature of the study of religion in a Catholic institution follows from the fact that in such schools theology or religious studies is related to, concentrates on, and even operates within a particular religious or faith tradition. That is, these schools do center their theological research and education on the Roman Catholic tradition. They pay special attention to the sources and the history of that particular faith tradition. They focus on the values that are characteristic of that religious family. These schools do this not only as a matter of fact; they do it explicitly and professedly.

To many critics, such a stance—that is, identification with a specific religious tradition—is inimical to and a violation of the spirit of academic work.[6] It is for this reason that many professionals refuse to take the theology work of the Catholic institution, whether graduate or undergraduate, seriously. They consider that such an adherence to a tradition could not result in anything but an extension of catechism or another form of the seminary. It seems to me, therefore, to be very important to show that such a stance, which is characteristic of the Catholic school, is in no way contrary to the true academic study of religion.

An academic institution or an academic program has the right to relate itself to one tradition, to one school of thought, to one facet of its area of study. A philosophy department can be analytic or existential or scholastic. An economics department can be quantitative or theoretical. A school of psychology can be clinically or research oriented. All of these are possible options within the scope of academic study.

Because an institution or a department exercises such an option, it cannot be judged non-academic. What we are pointing to here is what Quentin Quade, Dean of Marquette Universuty's graduate school, has called "legitimate academic alternatives."[7] No university or school can cover all the possible areas or orientations of a given subject. And none as a matter of fact does so. Each school makes selections of the concentration, the orientation, the scope of its work; it is such options which express the ideals and the value-system of the given school. The question is not whether there can be such an option, e.g., relation to a particular religious tradition. Rather, the critical question is what type of tradition one relates to and how the option is exercised. These are two key questions in the discussion of the relation between academic study and tradition. They are the factors which determine whether a program can be called academic.

Let us consider first the matter of the type of religius tradition. If one is examining the legitimacy, the academic legitimacy, of a Catholic institution relating to, concentrating on and even identifying with the Catholic tradition of Christianity, one must remember that religious tradition itself has always been most hospitable to and most compatible with the intellectual tradition represented by the university. Some religious traditions may be hostile to the very notion of scholarly study, to the rational investigation of their bases, their activities, etc. In those cases, it would be hard to project a department with an allegiance to such a tradition which would take an academic approach. But this is anything but true of the Roman Catholic tradition. The history of the *fidens quaerens intellectum* is much older than the expression itself, and also older than the western university. Therefore one could not say *a priori* that every religious tradition could have a university or an academic incorporation. If it were a tradition that were inimical to the intellect or to humanistic values, it would be difficult to imagine how this would relate to the academic work of the university or its department of religious studies except extrinsically, i.e., as an object of study. But e *converso*, this is the very reason why the central Catholic tradition in Christianity with its strong emphasis on the intellect, on the positive relation of nature and grace, on the nobility of man, etc., has always found the university a *locus* in which to incorporate and express itself. And thus this religious tradition seems particularly apt to be the center of an academic religious activity.

A second feature of the Catholic tradition which makes it a proper focus for academic work is its breadth or universality. One of the characteristic concerns of the academic study of religion is the breadth of man's religious experience, the multiplicity of the forms in which the search for the Transcendent appears. It is often these concerns which push programs toward the "religion in general" approach, or toward the purely formal treatment of religion. Here again a religious tradition which took a narrow, exclusivist stance could not deal with this very important and very legitimate human concern. But the central Catholic tradition of Christianity can. It has always understood that there was a universal dimension to its claims; it has always been concerned with the matter of the "universal salvific will"—though some expressions of this have been less felicitous than others! In contemporary Catholicism there is a very active, very powerful search for the means to relate the claims of Catholicism to other forms of man's religious activity.[8] The implication for the present discussion is that within the Catholic tradition itself, there is a base for the concern for the breadth of man's religious activity and expression. Thus one cannot legitimately object to the concentration on this tradition on the basis of its being indifferent or hostile to such a concern.

The second factor mentioned above as determinative of the academic character of a theology program is the manner in which the option for a "legitimate academic alternative" is exercised. By this is meant that the decision about the specific orientation of a department or program, the implementation of this in terms of curriculum, faculty recruitment, etc., must be made and carried out in a manner which is consonant with the accepted procedures of colleges and universities. The theology department cannot be regarded, either by the administration or by its faculty, as exempt from the general rules and requirements which govern other departments. The administration cannot expect to place people on the theology faculty or remove them from it without following the norms for recruitment and nonretention. The theology department cannot expect to act in the area of curriculum development or budget planning in an "exempt" manner. In their manner of exercising the academic option, the department of theology must also be academic; and in some cases this means changing present customs. The nature of the religious tradition to which one relates and the manner in which the academic option is exercised are thus two important factors in establishing the academic legitimacy of the theology or religious studies program.

4. Curriculum Considerations

There are three observations in the area of curriculum which I wish to make, even though they cannot be fully developed here.

It is often—in fact, commonly—argued that in order to be academic in the proper sense a religious studies department must be neutral, i.e., descriptive, phenomenological, non-committed. There is a presumption here of an inherent contradiction between an academic stance and a commitment to a value system, or at least to a religious value system.

I would argue that a department of theology or religious studies does not have to and, in the case of a Catholic institution, should not adopt such a stance. The course offerings of the department can be and should be varied. And by the term "varied" here I mean that it should include two types of courses, commitment courses and descriptive courses.[9] The focal point of this distinction is on the matter of truth claims. Any academic offering makes truth claims, whether it be in history or geography or theology. If in a theology course the truth claims are based upon the faith position of the one making the claim, then this is a commitment type course. For example: such assertions as Jesus Christ is God man; God is triune; Allah is the one true God. Such assertions must be distinguished from descriptive assertions. For example: Christians hold that Jesus Christ is the son of God; Mohammedans hold that Mohammed is the one true prophet of Allah. These statements are also truth claims, but they are not based on a faith position. They are descriptive of a faith position but they are based on study of historical documents, observation, etc.

It is not necessary that a department of theology offer only descriptive courses in order to be academic. It is perfectly legitimate to offer commitment courses in one's own or in other traditions, provided they are acknowledged and identified as such. A department of theology does not have to be "neutral" in order to be academic. A department in a Catholic institution may and I think should offer both types of courses. It does not have to adopt a neutral or non-committed stance. Commitment courses in the Catholic tradition should be offered since the university has its responsibility both for research and teaching to the religious tradition in which it stands. Descriptive courses, e.g., history of religious, philosophy of religion, phenomenology of religion, should be offered since they offer another mode of approach to the whole dimension of the religious, a dimension which is of interest and concern to the educated man and to the Catholic educated man. Also, the descriptive mode of treating the religious dimension seems to be more effective in many cases with the contemporary Catholic student.

Secondly, it is legitimate for a Catholic college or university to require theology or religious studies courses of its students. I have discussed this question at length elsewhere,[10] but I would like to review several points of the discussion here. In my opinion, a serious mistake has been made by some Catholic schools in recent years in dropping their academic theology requirements. I am not speaking here of cases in which schools dropped all academic course requirements in all departments. That is another case and must be discussed on other grounds. I am speaking about the many instances in which the specific course requirements for theology were dropped while biology, modern languages, etc., were retained. This action may have been taken for several motives: student distaste with poorly conceived and poorly taught courses, inability of the teachers in the theology area to develop an acceptable rationale for their work and its place in the overall work of their college. Some faculty in the theology area could not make the shift from custodial to academic rationales for their teaching.

I do not intend to repeat here the argument that I have worked out in detail in the article mentioned above, but the key elements are: 1) the right of the Catholic university to define itself in terms of a certain set of values, specifically those of the religious or spiritual dimension of man's existence; 2) the necessity of the university incorporating or expressing those values academically; 3) theological activity, both research and teaching, as a primary and essential mode of this academic expression of religious values; 4) therefore, the legitimacy of the requirement that the student body participate in this academic work, based on the direct relation between the ideal of man that the Catholic university professes and the formation of man which the university practices in an academic mode.

It is then legitimate for a school which has requirements expressing its educational ideas in other areas to have them also in the theology area. This is consistent with the self-definition of the university, with its spiritual and religious values, and with its academic mode of existence and expression.

Finally and very briefly, I would suggest that agreement on the importance of theology in the curriculum of the Catholic institution does not mean that the students must be given an over-all treatment of all truths of the Catholic faith. This curriculum posture is an imitation of the *summa* treatments of most seminaries. It has its place and function, but not for the undergraduate students. Educationally it would seem much more important that these students be given the opportunity to establish intellectual contact with some problems in the theology area, and to see some methods of theological reflection employed. Such selective contact is more likely to bring them alive to the nature of theological work, to the riches of the tradition in which they stand, to the importance of theology for their life decisions than is an exposure to a structured *summa* of theological truths, a *summa* which was developed in response to other programs in other times.

This is a secondary problem, but it is still a question for some administrators and faculty in Catholic institutions. The solution seems to me to come from reflection on the educational needs and the cultural situation of the student of today.

Conclusion

In this brief paper I have reflected on some of the elements which constitute the context for the discussion of the academic study of religion in the Catholic college or university. In my opinion, a number of poor options have been taken by theology departments in certain Catholic institutions because they have not reflected sufficiently on the specific context in which the academic study of religion in a Catholic school takes place. Among these poor options I would mention the notion that the department must be neutral in order to be academic, the posture that in the area of theology course requirements must be dropped, and the idea that the Catholic dimension of theology is best expressed by a potpourri faculty.

My own conclusions from the reflections which are suggested rather than fully developed in this brief paper would be several. First, academic does not mean neutral; it is entirely possible for a college or university to relate itself to a value system or a religious system and to do so academically. Secondly, a relation to a religious tradition such as Roman Catholicism can be a "legitimate academic alternative" for an institution of higher education. Thirdly, both the value system and the religious tradition must find expression which is academic and concrete, i.e., in terms of curriculum structures, faculty recruitment, etc.

And, finally, the rationale for the academic study of theology and the specific program which incorporates and expresses this rationale must be developed in context by the specific academic community of the given institution. There are common elements and common features; it is my hope that this paper has suggested some of them. But to be truly effective the rationale and the program must be worked out by those who are doing the teaching and learning in each Catholic college and university.

------

[1]The term "university" is used here to cover both the university and the college. As will be obvious from the discussion, the focus in this essay is on the undergraduate study of religion, not on graduate teaching and research, which has a distinctive rationale.

[2]See The Study of Religion in College and Universities, ed. by Paul Ramsey and John F. Wilson, Princeton, N.J.: Princeton University Press, 1970. This book is the latest of a long series of studies on this question. It is particularly valuable for its "Introduction," which gives the historical background of the discussion of this question in American higher education and for the "Selected Bibliography," which is an annotated listing of the major works in this area since 1928.

[3]For example, John F. Wilson, "Introduction," op. cit. p. 15.

[4]Clyde Holbrook, Religion: A Humanistic Field, Englewood Cliffs, N.J.: Prentice-Hall, 1963.

[5]"Theology and The Jesuit College: A New Rationale," Privately printed in the report of the 1969 JEA Denver Workshop entitled Guidelines for Jesuit Higher Education.

[6]Cf. the essay of Victor Preller, "Catholic Studies in the University" in the Princeton volume cited above in note 2 (pp. 139-158).

[7]This concept is used and explained by Quade in "Academic Planning and Leadership: Problems and Potentials of Catholic Universities," College Newsletter, Vol. XXXIII, No. 2, December 1970, pp. 3-5, and in an unpublished paper, "University and Catholic: Final Report of the Special Committee on the Christian Character of Marquette University."
Quade has also written a brief but very perceptive article which explains the perspective which is presented in the two papers mentioned above: Quentin L. Quade, "The Catholic University: A Christian Perspective," America, Vol. 120, No. 14, (Apr. 5, 1969) pp. 392-96.

[8]See the work of Karl Rahner, H. R. Schlette, Eugene Frick, and others.

[9]See the discussion of this distinction in my study, "Theology Should Be Required of All," in New Dimensions in Religious Experience, ed. George Devine, Staten Island, N.Y.: Alba House, 1971, pp. 311 ff.

[10]Ibid., p. 301-313.

Part II
The Present Scene:
A Summary Account

The Present Scene: A Summary Account

1. Growth in Undergraduate Religious Studies, 1950-1970

It has been widely held that during the decades following the second World War there was a veritable explosion in the academic study of religion at the college and university level, so that religious studies developed at a more rapid rate even than the overall expansion of higher education. Is this true?

The answer to the question can be either yes or no, depending entirely on the kind of institution being considered, particularly whether church-related or public or private non-sectarian. If one were to lump all types of institutions together, it would appear that the academic study of religion has expanded in students and faculty at about the same rate as college enrollments and faculties generally. But that would be greatly misleading, for strikingly divergent trends have characterized the different types of institutions. The true picture can be exhibited both (a) with respect to the establishment of religion programs, and (b) with respect to the expansion in enrollment and faculty.

a. It is hardly surprising that church-related institutions were the first to establish formal programs in religion for schools from which information is available concerning the date of the first full-time appointment in religion, the sequence of development is clear: Protestant church-related institutions were first, followed by Roman Catholic schools, private non-sectarian colleges, and finally public institutions. As Table 1 shows, almost half of the Protestant

---

Table 1*

INSTITUTIONAL AFFILIATION IN RELATION TO THE TIME OF FIRST FULL-TIME FACULTY APPOINTMENT IN RELIGION

by percent of institutions with full programs, 1969-1970

Date of First Full-Time Appointment in Religion	Institutional Affiliation			
			Private	
	Protestant	Catholic	Non-Sect.	Public
	%	%	%	%
Before 1909	47	13	26	3
1909-1940	34	49	18	7
Since 1940	19	38	56	90
	100	100	100	100
	(N=29)	(N=50)	(N=55)	(N=146)

Based on information from 280 institutions now offering an undergraduate major in religion.

related institutions made their first full-time faculty appointment in religion before 1909, and by 1940 over four-fifths had at least one full-time religion faculty member. Full-time appointments in Roman Catholic schools came somewhat later, partly because many of these institutions were themselves established later than the Protestant church-related schools. Only 13% of the Roman Catholic schools had a full-time religion faculty member before 1909, but nearly half of them made such an appointment between 1909 and 1940.

In private non-sectarian colleges, however, although a quarter had faculty members teaching full-time in religion before 1909, the majority did not make a full-time appointment until after 1940. And in public institutions, 90% of such appointments were made after 1940.

The development of religion programs in the public sector is more recent even, than Table 1 shows. A fuller investigation of the dates of origin of religion programs in public colleges and universities shows that of 96 organized programs of religious studies, ten were in existence in 1930 (mostly in Southern universities), seven were established in the 1930's, eight in the 1940's, ten in the 1950's, seventeen in the first half of the next decade, and forty-four between 1966 and 1970. In other words, almost two-thirds of these institutions inaugurated their programs in the 1960's, with the major explosion coming in the latter half of the decade. Without question a major factor in this development was the U.S. Supreme Court decision in the Schempp case (1963), which has been widely interpreted to have made explicit the constitutional propriety of the academic study of religion at all levels in U.S. public education.[2]

A similar pattern of development is evident with respect to changes made within the structures of religion programs. In response to questions concerning the date of establishment of religion programs in their present structures, almost 40% of the Protestant church-related institutions reported that their present program structures antedated 1940, whereas at least four-fifths of the programs in Roman Catholic, private non-sectarian, and public institutions were organized in their present form since 1940. It is noteworthy that not only in public institutions, but also in Roman Catholic schools have the religion programs been restructured significantly in the 1960's. Forty-three per cent of the Roman Catholic institutions reported that the present structure of their religion program was established after 1965. The basic patterns in private non-sectarian institutions were mostly established between 1940 and 1964.

b. Enrollment and faculty expansion patterns have also varied greatly in different types of institutions. Enrollment data, particularly in specific subject areas, are notoriously difficult to secure for any extended period of time. Information has been obtained from departmental offices, however, for enrollments in religion courses, compared with the total undergraduate enrollments in the institutions, for the Fall terms in 1954, 1959, 1964 and 1969 — in a representative group of 167 institutions: 104 Protestant-related, 36 Roman Catholic and 27 private non-sectarian. Since so many of the religion programs in public institutions are of recent origin, extensive information would not exist for such a long period, but reports are available from 38 public institutions for the five-year period 1964-1969. See Table 2.

As Table 2 makes clear, patterns of religion enrollments in the various types of institutions have been diverse both in the proportions of students studying religion and in the relative changes in those proportions.

For example, in 1959, almost three-fourths of the students in Roman Catholic institutions were enrolled in religion courses (this was the high point in the years reported), as compared with slightly less than one-third in Protestant church-related institutions, 8.6% in private, non-sectarian institutions, and only 3.4% in the public institutions with religion programs.[3] Obviously the vast majority of students in undergraduate religion programs have been in church-related institutions. (It is also true, of course, that most of the programs are in church-related institutions — see Section 2 below.)

Equally important have been the dramatic changes in the proportions. In Protestant-related schools, for example, the number of students taking religion courses increased at approximately the same rate as the institutions as a whole between 1954 and 1964, but for the following five years at a much slower rate, so that over the whole fifteen-year period religion enrollments increased only 53%, whereas the total number of undergraduates increased 75%, and the ratio of religion enrollments to total student body declined from 33% in 1954 to 29% in 1969.

In Roman Catholic institutions, the religion enrollments actually increased more rapidly than the total undergraduate population between 1954 and 1959, but then at a rate for the next five years slower than the total institutional growth, and after 1964 the actual numbers of students enrolled in religion courses declined, so that by 1969 there were almost exactly the same number as a decade earlier. Thus over the whole fifteen years, religion course enrollments increased by 31%, whereas the total number of undergraduates in Roman Catholic schools increased by 82%. The ratio of religion enrollments to total student body declined from 69% to 50%.

In both Protestant and Roman Catholic institutions, the relatively slower growth in religion enrollments is to be explained partly by the elimination or drastic reduction of religion requirements, particularly in many Roman Catholic institutions after the Second Vatican Council. Data available from a total of 409 institutions that have had religious requirements indicate that 172 of them have reduced or abandoned requirements (compared with 19 that

Table 2

ENROLLMENTS IN UNDERGRADUATE RELIGION COURSES IN RELATION TO TOTAL UNDERGRADUATE STUDENT BODIES

Fall Terms 1954-1969

	1954	1959	1964	1969	Increase 1954-1969 %
A. 104 Protestant-related Institutions					
Number of undergraduates	78,250	94,933	117,467	137,932	75
Religion course enrollments	25,704	30,915	37,232	39,438	53
Ratio of religion enrollments to total student body	33%	32.6%	32%	29%	
B. 36 Roman Catholic Institutions					
Number of undergraduates	33,173	41,048	52,510	60,265	82
Religion course enrollments	22,767	29,886	33,649	29,915	31
Ratio of religion enrollments to total student body	69%	73%	64%	50%	
C. 27 Private Non-sectarian Institutions					
Number of undergraduates	52,001	58,301	67,254	77,098	48
Religion course enrollments	3,798	4,986	5,871	8,523	124
Ratio of religion enrollments to total student body	7%	8.6%	8.7%	11%	
D. 25 Public Institutions (1964-1969)					
Number of Undergraduates	—	—	169,300	262,900	55
Religion course enrollments			5,697	14,373	150
Ratio of religion enrollments to total student body			3.4%	5.5%	

have increased their requirements). A few Roman Catholic institutions showed declines from 100% of the students enrolled in religion courses in 1959 to less than 20% in 1969. In view of the extensive reductions in requirements, it is on the whole remarkable that religion enrollments have in many instances continued to climb.

The fifteen-year pattern of growth in private non-sectarian institutions has been quite different from that in church-related schools. Here the rate of increase in religion enrollments has been much more rapid than that of the undergraduate enrollments as a whole, particularly during the 1964-1969 period. Over the whole fifteen-year period, religion enrollments grew two and a half times as fast as total enrollments, i.e., 124% as compared with 48%. Thus the ratio of religion enrollments to total student body increased from 7% to 11%.

In public institutions, for the brief span about which sufficient information is available, the relatively greater rate of growth in religion enrollments has been even more notable. Twenty-five public institutions that had organized religion programs in 1964 showed a rate of increase in religion course enrollments, 1964-1969, that was nearly triple the increase in total undergraduate population (150% as compared with 55%). Consequently the proportion of students taking religion courses, while much smaller than in private non-sectarian and especially church-related schools, increased relatively more rapidly than in any of the other types of institutions, i.e., from 3.4% to 5.5%. Thus in 1969, approximately one out of twenty students in these public institutions was enrolled in one or more religion courses, as compared with one out of every nine students in the private non-sectarian institutions with religion programs.

Patterns of expansion in religion faculties have been more or less like those in enrollment. It is noteworthy, however, that Roman Catholic religion faculties continued to increase between 1964 and 1969, even though the enrollments in religion courses fell. Furthermore, religion faculty in Protestant-related institutions seem to have grown at a slightly more rapid rate than religion enrollments in those institutions (a 65% increase between 1954 and 1969, as compared with 53% increase in religion enrollments).

In both public and private non-sectarian institutions, it appears that faculty expansion has not kept pace with the increase in undergraduate religion enrollments, particularly during the latter half of the 1960's. In private non-sectarian institutions, religion course enrollments increased by 45% between 1964 and 1969, while the number of faculty increased only 25%. In public institutions, religion enrollments increased by 150%, whereas the increase in religion faculty was only 46%.

2. The Present Distribution of Religion Programs

In what types of institutions are organized programs for the academic study of religion most likely to be found?

In view of our sketch of the growth of religion programs, it is not surprising to discover that religious affiliation of institutions is the single most significant factor in accounting for the presence of a program or department of religious studies. As Table 3 shows nearly all Protestant and Roman Catholic institutions have programs of religious studies, though there is an important difference between Roman Catholic and Protestant schools as to whether an undergraduate major is offered. Most of these programs, as we saw, were established before the Second World War. Yet it is also striking that by 1970 almost half of the private non-sectarian institutions and almost a third of the public four-year colleges and universities had programs. By 1970, therefore, with the rapid growth of the previous half decade, the study of religion had become significantly, even though not yet massively established in public higher education. There are actually more religion programs in public institutions (29% of 423) than in private non-sectarian institutions (47% of 213). There is no evidence as yet that this trend toward expansion of religious studies in public institutions has ended, although the severe budgetary restrictions on public higher education necessarily tend to restrict development of all new programs.

Table 3*

RELIGION PROGRAMS IN RELATION TO
INSTITUTIONAL AFFILIATION, 1969-1970

Type of Religion Program	Public %	Private Non-Sectarian %	Roman Catholic %	Protestant %
Full Program, i.e., Undergraduate major offered	12	30	34	71
Program but no major	15	13	40	9
†Program Unspecified	2	4	18	13
No Program but Religion Courses offered	28	16	6	7
No Religion courses offered	43	37	2	0
	100	100	100	100
	(N=423)	(N=213)	(N=250)	(N=346)

*This tabulation does not include 87 schools of other affiliations—Jewish, nondenominational Protestant, and unclassified—most of which (71%) reported a religion program of some sort.

†Includes schools that, in response to the screening questionnaire, indicated the existence of a special program or department of religion, but that either did not respond to subsequent questionnaires or neglected to provide information on the type of program.

54

Table 4 shows the proportions of institutions in various regions of the United States and Canada having organized religion programs. As might be expected, religion programs are more highly concentrated in those geographical areas where church-related institutions are most common.

Table 4

RELIGION PROGRAMS IN RELATION TO GEOGRAPHICAL AREA, 1969-1970

Geographical Area	Percentage of Institutions having a Religion Program
North Central	74%
South Atlantic	68%
Extra Continental U.S.	67%
Middle Atlantic	62%
South Central	62%
Pacific	57%
Canada	53%
New England	46%
Mountain	46%

The U.S. areas are classified according to the census divisions: *New England:* Maine, New Hampshire, Vermont, Massachusetts, Rhode Island, Connecticut. *Middle Atlantic:* Pennsylvania, New Jersey, New York. *South Atlantic:* West Virginia, Maryland, Delaware, Virginia, North Carolina, South Carolina, Georgia, Florida, District of Columbia. *North Central* (East): Wisconsin, Illinois, Indiana, Michigan, Ohio. (West): North Dakota, South Dakota, Nebraska, Kansas, Minnesota, Iowa, Missouri. *South Central* (East): Kentucky, Tennessee, Alabama, Mississippi. (West): Texas, Louisiana, Oklahoma, Arkansas. *Mountain:* Montana, Idaho, Wyoming, Utah, Colorado, Arizona, New Mexico. *Pacific:* California, Oregon, Washington, Alaska. *Extra-Continental United States:* Hawaii, Virgin Islands, Puerto Rico, Guam.

Table 5 shows the proportions of institutions of varying sizes having religion programs. Again, the variations here are probably not unrelated to religious affiliation since the public institutions, with a smaller percentage of religion programs, tend to be the largest in student population.

Table 5

SIZE OF INSTITUTION IN RELATION TO RELIGION PROGRAM, 1969-1970

Number of Undergraduates	Percentage of Institutions with Program
750 or fewer	70%
751-1250	76%
1251-2570	64%
Over 2750	50%

Again, as Tables 6 and 7 show, religion programs tend to be concentrated in liberal arts institutions, particularly in autonomous liberal arts schools, many of which are church-related. Table 6 shows the percentage of colleges of various types having religion programs. Table 7 shows the distribution of religion programs among these types of institutions, in relation to the total distribution of such colleges among all United States four-year institutions of higher education. Again the concentration in autonomous liberal arts colleges is noteworthy: whereas only 43% of the four-year institutions are autonomous liberal arts schools, 56% of the religion programs are found in these schools. On the other hand, whereas among the 20% of all institutions classified as "other," only 11% of the religion programs are found (the category "other" includes largely technical and professional schools, and a few schools of religion).

One further variable is important to note in relation to the distribution of programs of religious studies, namely, institutional quality. It appears that, second to religious affiliation, the presence of a religion program is most strongly associated with the academic quality of an institution. The higher the quality the greater the

---

Table 6

TYPE OF COLLEGE IN RELATION TO RELIGION PROGRAM,
1969-1970

Type of College	Percentage with a Religion Program
Autonomous Liberal Arts	85%
Liberal Arts in University	65%
Teachers College	51%
Other	35%

Table 7

DISTRIBUTION OF RELIGION PROGRAMS IN RELATION
TO THE DISTRIBUTION OF TYPES OF COLLEGES

Type of College	Percent of Total Institutions %	Percent of Religion Programs %
Autonomous Liberal Arts	43	56
Liberal Arts in University	20	20
Teachers College	17	13
Other	20	11
	100	100

likelihood of there being a program of religion. This appears from two comparative studies, one using Cass and Birnbaum's ratings of institutions according to selectivity in admissions, and the other using the resource index score developed by George Nash in a study made from the Bureau of Applied Social Research, Columbia University.[4]

From these comparisons, it is evident that the more selective institutions are more likely to have undergraduate religion programs. Seventy-nine percent of the schools ranked by Cass and Birnbaum in the top selectivity group (i.e., most selective, very selective, and highly selective) have an organized religion program, whereas only 57% of the schools not rated for selectivity have programs. Furthermore, among those institutions with a program, the more selective schools are more likely to offer an undergraduate major in religion.

A similar result emerges when Nash's Resource Index, which is a measure of institutional resources per student, is used as a measure of institutional quality. Overall, in those schools ranked as high resource institutions (i.e., the top 13%) 85% have a religion program, whereas among the low resource schools (the bottom 21%) only 40% have a religion program. Furthermore, high rankings are correlated with the presence of a full program in contrast to a partial program.

This correlation should not be unexpected, since high resource schools are able to offer more varied programs of all sorts. But since church-related schools have such a high incidence of religion programs (93-94%), it is important to note that the correlation with the resource index scores holds for both public and private non-sectarian colleges. The patterns are shown in Tables 8 and 9.

Table 8

RELIGION PROGRAMS IN RELATION TO THE RESOURCE INDEX
SCORES OF PUBLIC INSTITUTIONS

Type of Program	Resource Index Scores				
	High	Upper Middle	Lower Middle	Low	Total
	%	%	%	%	%
Full Program	37	23	5	5	12
Partial Programs	9	15	15	16	16
Unspecified Programs	0	8	5	6	4
Religion courses but no program	27	33	31	24	29
No Religion courses offered	27	21	44	49	39
	100	100	100	100	100
	(N=22)	(N=65)	(N=99)	(N=96)	(N=282)

Table 9

RELIGION PROGRAMS IN RELATION TO THE RESOURCE INDEX SCORES OF PRIVATE INSTITUTIONS

Type of Program	Resource Index Scores				
	High	Upper-Middle	Lower-Middle	Low	Total
	%	%	%	%	%
Full Program	66	19	29	11	38
Partial Program	15	11	21	6	14
Unspecified Programs	11	4	11	5	9
Religion courses but no program	6	19	18	28	15
No Religion courses offered	2	47	21	50	24
	100	100	100	100	100
	(N=46)	(N=27)	(N=28)	(N=18)	(N=119)

3. The Goals of Organized Religion Programs

The purposes of the study of religion in college and university have been undergoing marked redefinition in the decades following World War II. Religion has come increasingly to be looked upon as a significant field of study within the liberal arts curriculum, rather than (a) a subject so bound up with the evangelistic and confessional interests of the religious communities that it could not be dealt with responsibly in the academic world, or (b) a means of caring for the souls of students during their undergraduate careers. That is, religion has been established as an "academic discipline" — not in the sense of having a methodology distinct from all others, but as a major area of human experience that needs to be identified for special study.

This change is particularly evident, of course, in the growth of programs of religious studies in the independent and public colleges and universities. These programs are pluralistic in faculty, they have no intent to prepare students for clerical careers and they eschew both evangelistic and pastoral goals. But related changes have been taking place in church-related institutions as well. Formerly, religion programs were often viewed as preludes to theological seminary studies, or as direct professional preparation of religious education workers, or as religious training of laity. The dominant reasons for the inclusion of religion courses (and requirements) in the curriculum of church-related institutions were often "evangelical" or "catechetical," that is, they were intended to convert or instruct in the faith and thus to provide support for commitment to the religious community and a religious and moral basis for life. (These were, of course, also precisely the reasons why, in many private as well as public institutions in the decades following the first World War, there was a strong reaction against the study of religion.) These motives were also important in the establishment of the numerous schools of religion adjacent to college and university campuses. Increasingly, however, except in the religiously conservative institutions, such purposes are being rapidly abandoned in favor of quite different understandings of the roles of religious studies, and the patterns of study are changing accordingly. Religion is viewed as a field within the humanities or social sciences whose study is justified simply by its contribution to any liberal education that proposes to take into account the whole range of human experience. Correlatively, as we have already noted, religion requirements have been reduced or abandoned at an increasingly rapid rate. In part, some of these changes are associated with the increasing secularization of private colleges. But even in institutions seeking to maintain close ties to the religious communities, the departments of "theology" or "religious education" or "Bible" with their former confessional and/or professional orientation, are being transformed into programs that are at least trans-confessional or ecumenical or pluralistic.[5]

We should not exaggerate, of course, the extent of these changes. Important differences remain among types of institutions. Table 10 and Figure 1 show the relative weights assigned by department chairmen to seven different possible aims of undergraduate religion programs. These reflect reports from the 385 institutions, all of which offered an undergraduate major in religion. The respondents were asked to indicate, for each stated purpose, whether this goal was "of no importance," "somewhat important," or "highly important." Responses of "highly important" were assigned a value of 4.0, responses of "somewhat important" a value of 2.0, and responses indicating "no importance" a value of 0.0.

In both Table 10 and Figure 1 the aims have been listed in overall decreasing importance, as reported by departmental chairmen. Not only for the whole population, but for every type of institution (with the exception of conservative Protestant schools, where the differences are slight) the most important aim was the providing of factual and analytical understanding of religion. But as one moves on to the other aims, there emerges a greater diversity among the various types of institutions, except that all assign a relatively similar importance to the preparation of undergraduates for graduate study in religion.[6] It is important to recall in this connection that all these institutions offer an undergraduate major. Preparation for graduate study would doubtless be a far less explicit aim of programs that did not offer an undergraduate major.

The patterns of importance in public and in private non-sectarian institutions parallel each other closely. (And the differences would be even less but for the fact that some institutions that classified themselves as private non-sectarian are of conservative Protestant orientation, though with no particular denominational affiliation.) For most public institutions, the goal of nourishing commitment to religious faith, either that of a particular religious tradition or "a religious faith of some sort" and the goal of developing

Table 10

AIMS OF RELIGION PROGRAMS

In Relation to Religious Affiliation of Institutions

Aims	Total (385)	Public (36)	Private Non-Sect. (60)	Roman Catholic (63)	Liberal Protestant (111)	Conservative Protestant (81)	Other (34)
Providing factual and analytical understanding of religion	3.73	3.86	3.83	3.47	3.80	3.77	3.73
Giving students a sympathetic understanding of a wide range of religious traditions and cultures	3.41	3.86	3.61	3.05	3.43	3.34	3.04
Development of concern for values	3.37	2.72	3.02	3.47	3.31	3.87	3.44
Preparing students for graduate study in religion	2.53	2.48	2.67	2.15	2.64	2.68	2.70
Nourishment of commitment to a religious faith of some sort	2.36	.99	1.73	2.40	2.31	3.13	2.83
Development of church leadership	2.11	.56	1.43	1.85	2.17	2.96	3.01
Nourishment of students' commitment to a particular religious tradition	1.50	.42	1.02	2.74	.84	2.04	2.31

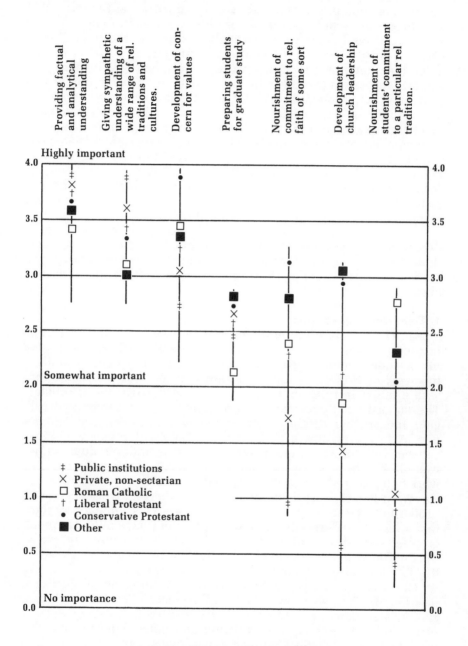

AIMS OF RELIGION PROGRAMS
In relation to Religious Affiliation of Institutions

Figure 1

church leadership, are counted as of no importance. Similarly, liberal Protestant schools assign a very low value to the nourishing of religious commitment to a particular religious tradition. Roman Catholic institutions, on the contrary, count this as a matter of considerable importance. Conservative Protestant institutions are somewhat less concerned with the cultivation of commitment to a particular religious tradition, but much more concerned with the nourishment of religious faith in general and with the development of church leadership. Roman Catholic religion programs rate the development of church leadership of less importance than Protestant or "other" institutions, because traditionally the development of church leadership in Roman Catholicism has been the responsibility of special seminaries for the training of priests, rather than of liberal arts institutions, the latter having rather the responsibility of the religious training of the laity.

Again, however, it should be emphasized that the spectrum of departmental purposes exhibited in Table 10 and Figure 1 is only those reported in the Spring of 1970 and thus represents a cross section at a particular point in the processes of change described above.

4. Departmental Profiles

a. The typical undergraduate religion program, particularly in institutions where an undergraduate major is offered, is located in an independent department of religion (or religious studies, theology, or Bible). As Table 11 shows, in 60% of the institutions with a major in religion, there is a distinct department of religion. The majority of the remainder are combined departments of religion and another discipline, most commonly religion and philosophy. A few programs are offered by schools of religion within a college. Only one institution reported that its undergraduate major was offered by a school of religion adjacent to the university, its work being accredited by the university.

What is most surprising in Table 11 is the relatively very small proportion of interdepartmental structures. This appears to show that although undergraduate religion programs have not infrequently been started as interdepartmental courses of study supervised by interdepartmental committees, they have regularly moved to the status of distinct administrative and budgetary units. This is to speak, of course, only of administrative structure, not of curricula (see Part III, below). It does not at all reflect the extent to which a student's academic program may involve cross-disciplinary work or formal joint majors between religion and other departments. The predominance of distinct religion departments may indicate that, in this area of study as in others, education has gone the way of increasing departmentalization, specialization, isolation, etc. But it is much more likely to reflect the practical needs of organizing the educational establishment for budgetary and administrative pur-

Table 11

ORGANIZATIONAL FORM OF RELIGION PROGRAMS

	Schools with Undergraduate Majors %	Schools with Partial Programs %
Department of Religion (or Religious Studies or Theology)	60	50
Combined Department of Religion and other Discipline (e.g., Religion and Philosophy)	32	32
School of Religion within the college or university	3	0
School of Religion adjacent to college or university whose work is accredited by college	*	1
Interdepartmental Program	1	5
Other (primarily Bible Colleges)	3	12
	99	100
	(N = 390)	(N = 222)

*A single school responded to this category

poses. Educational programs and patterns grow in colleges and universities only if they are tended, and that requires their being given an organizing center, structure, a budget, some appointive control, and so forth. This is plainly the case with respect to programs of religious studies. Those that have been organized simply as interdepartmental or interdisciplinary structures have regularly failed to prosper.[7]

b. The typical religion faculty is modest in size, as indicated in Table 12, which portrays the overall distribution of departmental faculty sizes for 633 schools, distinguishing between those with an undergraduate major and those without. The median number of faculty for the full-program institutions was 5.7, for the partial program institutions it was 4.2 faculty members. The very largest faculties reported here are almost entirely in large Roman Catholic institutions, where there have been extensive requirements of religion courses and correspondingly large faculties. Yet at the other extreme, while even among institutions offering an undergraduate major, there were 42 that had only two faculty members and four schools that somehow managed with only one, such small departments are relatively rare. They are most common, of course, in institutions with only partial programs. But the development of undergraduate major programs has been accompanied not only by gross faculty expansion in relation to enrollment, but also apparently by recognition of the variety of sub-fields within religion and the need for differing faculty specialties.

c. From the data shown in Table 13 it is evident that the great

Table 12

RELIGION FACULTY SIZE IN RELATION TO TYPES OF
PROGRAMS (Fall 1969)

Number of Faculty	Numbers of Schools			
	Full Program	Partial Program	Not Classified	Total
More than 20	13	1	0	14
16-20	16	2	1	19
13-15	16	2	3	21
11-12	24	5	2	31
9-10	28	11	1	40
8	26	10	0	36
7	28	12	1	41
6	49	8	2	59
5	51	16	1	68
4	80	29	5	114
3	53	29	0	82
2	42	29	2	73
1	4	28	3	35
Total:	430	182	21	633

majority of religion faculty members hold full-time academic appointments — 81% of those in full programs, 69% of those in partial
programs. The dominant pattern is that of appointment to teach
full-time in the religion department, but it is significant that slightly
less than half of all the religion faculty were reported to hold a full-
time appointment only within the religion department. As might be
expected from the proportion of combined religion and philosophy
departments, joint appointments for faculty in religion and philosophy form the next most common pattern (12% in the full programs
and 16% in the partial programs). Smaller numbers of faculty hold
joint appointments with history, social science or language departments. In the full-program schools a total of 6.5% hold joint appointments with divinity school or graduate theological departments.

The combination of teaching in religion programs with the
exercise of some form of pastoral responsibility continues to be
frequent. Eleven percent of the faculty serve as chaplains, campus
ministers, or ministers of parishes. More important, perhaps, is the
fact that in the 633 institutions reporting, there were 179 faculty
who served as college chaplains in addition to teaching in the religion programs. Assuming that only rarely would there be two chaplains in the same college, this means that in almost 30% of the
institutions surveyed, the chaplain participated in the work of the
religion faculty. Teaching by chaplains or by campus ministers,

parish ministers and others engaged in ministerial activity—is also plainly more common in the institutions not offering an undergraduate major in religion. These combinations, of course, are almost entirely to be found in church-related institutions, occasionally in private non-sectarian institutions, but rarely in public institutions— although some public institutions grant academic credit for religion work offered by adjacent schools of religion or by incumbents of Bible chairs supported by religious communities. The combination of Chaplaincy-teaching appears to characterize slightly less than half the church-related schools.[8]

    d. It seems that religion faculty are unusually heavily involved in administrative responsibilities. This is in part, of course, a consequence of the modest size of departments. Since the average religion department has five faculty members it is to be expected that one in five religion teachers served as chairman of his department

---

Table 13

COLLEGE (UNIVERSITY) STATUS

	Full Program %	Partial Program %	Total %	Total N
Full time faculty				
In Religion Dept. only	51.5	35.7	47.8	(1,749)
In Religion *and*				
Philosophy	12.1	16.5	13.1	(479)
History	1.5	2.6	1.8	(67)
Social Sciences	2.1	1.9	2.1	(77)
Language	2.1	2.6	2.2	(81)
Divinity School	1.8	1.4	2.0	(95)
Graduate Theology	4.7	1.9	4.0	(147)
Other	4.8	6.6	5.2	(190)
Part time faculty and				
College chaplain	4.4	6.6	4.8	(179)
Campus Minister	0.9	3.7	1.5	(56)
Parish Minister	1.8	3.2	2.1	(77)
Other outside ministerial				
duties	2.2	4.5	2.7	(98)
Member of faculty of				
other institution	3.9	5.5	4.2	(154)
Other	6.1	6.8	6.3	(233)
	99.9	99.5	99.8	

Based on reports from 633 institutions, with 3,662 religion faculty identified as to faculty status.

or program (see Table 14). What is surprising, however, is the number of faculty involved in other major administrative responsibilities. As Table 14 shows, these involve altogether another 20% of the religion faculty. An unusually high proportion seem to be engaged in general college or university administration. Of the total of 2,511 faculty about whom such information is available, 183 were engaged in general college administration as well as teaching. The individuals constitute only 7.2% of the total faculty, but they may be involved in general administration in as many as 30% of the 633 institutions represented.

e. Faculty and Enrollment. Religion departments have the reputation of being strongly oriented toward teaching. Whether this reputation is deserved, we have no proper means of assessing. But the extent of teaching responsibilities may be judged from a glance at the varying enrollment ranges in religion programs. Table 15 shows the percentages of institutions, full-program and partial-program, having religion enrollments in the ranges indicated during the Fall term 1969.

A comparison of student/faculty ratios, in schools with varying sizes of religion enrollment, is more significant. Table 16 makes clear that there is a general deterioration in student/faculty ratio with increase in departmental enrollment. The table shows the range in the number of students registered in religion courses per faculty member, the mean average and the median ratios, in the institutions of different types for which adequate information was available. The ratios are calculated from total undergraduate registration in religion courses for the Fall term 1969, in relation to full-time faculty equivalents (each part-time faculty member being counted as one-half). These ratios do not, of course, indicate class sizes, since each faculty member was teaching two or three or per-

---

Table 14

PERCENTAGES OF RELIGION FACULTY HAVING
ADMINISTRATIVE DUTIES

	%	N
Chairman or Director of Religion Department	21.4	(538)
Chairman or Director of other department	5.1	(128)
Chairman or Director of Undergraduate or Graduate Religion Programs	3.1	(77)
Chairman or Director of Other Undergraduate or Graduate Programs	2.2	(55)
General University (College) Administrator	7.2	(183)
No administrative duties	53.0	(1,330)
Other	8.0	(200)
	100.0	

Table 15

RELIGION DEPARTMENT ENROLLMENTS

Fall 1969

Enrollment Ranges	Public	Percent of Institutions Private Non-Sect.	Roman Catholic	Protestant	Total	
	%	%	%	%	%	N
0-124	32	32	19	13	20.7	126
125-249	22	22	14	31	23.6	144
250-374	8	21	17	20	17.3	105
375-499	8	13	10	14	11.7	71
500-749	11	7	14	12	11.7	71
750-999	9	2	7.5	3	5.1	31
1000-1499	8	2	7.5	3.5	5.1	31
1500-more	2	1	11	3.5	4.9	30
	100	100	100	100.0	100.1	609
	(N=100)	(N=95)	(N=160)	(N=254)		

haps more classes. But they do indicate the average number of students in religion courses for which each faculty member was responsible.

The very small departments (those with fewer than 125 students) should be ignored perhaps in this comparison, since these often represent either new programs or very small institutions. But it is important to note that the average faculty member in institutions with religion enrollments greater than 1,020 was teaching twice as many students as his counterpart in departments with enrollments between 125 and 252. Over all, as enrollment increases, so does the ratio of students to faculty. It also appears that instructors in public institutions, particularly in the middle enrollment ranges, have heavier student loads than their colleagues in other types of institutions.[9] Again, this reflects in part that faculty expansion in the public institutions has not kept pace with increasing enrollments.

5. Curriculum

a. Patterns of requirements. We noted earlier that many colleges have in recent years reduced or abandoned required courses in religion. It should also be noted, however, that the larger proportion of church-related institutions still maintain some requirement for the study of religion by all undergraduates. Among 374 institutions that offered an undergraduate major, 65% reported in the Spring of 1970 that there was some requirement of course work in religion. Thirty-five percent of the schools had a requirement of one or two religion courses for graduation, another 15% required three to five courses, and the remaining 15% required six or more religion courses of all students.

Table 16

RATIOS OF ENROLLMENT TO FACULTY
IN RELIGION DEPARTMENTS, FALL 1969

Departmental Enrollments	Student/Faculty Ratios		
	Range	Mean	Median
Over 1,020			
Public (N=10)	54-300	118	147
Private (N=2)	102-162	142	
Catholic (N=11)	91-356	138	112
Protestant (N=9)	96-550	132	136
509-1,020			
Public (N=12)	83-278	126	118
Private (N=8)	29-191	71	86
Catholic (N=10)	71-214	94	86
Protestant (N=12)	70-183	109	129
253-508			
Public (N=11)	53-210	101	105
Private (N=16)	20-230	75	84
Catholic (N=8)	37-143	74	76
Protestant (N=48)	45-257	85	82
125-252			
Public (N=9)	51-111	62	67
Private (N=13)	38-100	60	57
Catholic (N=8)	26-111	52	53
Protestant (N=40)	21-189	62	66
0-124			
Public (N=10)	9-200	32	34
Private (N=10)	8-77	31	30
Catholic (N=5)	6-75	17	33
Protestant (N=19)	8-94	28	26

Such requirements are found almost entirely, of course, in church-related or religiously oriented institutions, as is shown in Table 17. The most extensive religion requirements are naturally found in Roman Catholic and Conservative Protestant institutions. It should also be noted that some of the institutions identifying themselves as private non-sectarian are non-denominational schools with a strong religious orientation, usually Protestant, and that the institutions classified as "other" are mainly religiously oriented institutions.

Among schools with no religion requirement, most provide a place for the study of religion as a part of general education or distributional requirements. Of the schools offering an undergraduate major, 14% reported not having distributional requirements at all. But among schools that do have such requirements, five out

Table 17

NUMBER OF RELIGION COURSES REQUIRED OF ALL STUDENTS

By Types of Institutions

Number of Religion Courses Required of all Students	Religious Affiliation of Institution					
	Public Non-Sect.	Private Non-Sect.	Roman Catholic	Liberal Protestant	Cons. Protestant	Other
	%	%	%	%	%	%
None Required	100	76	22	32	9	7
One or Two Required	0	5	25	56	44	45
At Least Three Required	0	19	52	13	47	48
	(33)	(59)	(63)	(110)	(78)	(31)

of six (83%) include religion courses among those that can be taken to satisfy the requirement.[10]

b. The undergraduate major. Of all the four-year institutions reporting a special undergraduate program in religion, approximately two-thirds offer a religion major.[11] We saw earlier that religious affiliation is presently the single most important factor in accounting for the presence of an organized program for the academic study of religion. Religious affiliation is in a somewhat different way a factor in determining whether the religion program includes an undergraduate major. For 812 institutions with a program in 1970, where religious affiliation was reported, Table 18 shows the distribution of types of programs. (See also Table 3, above).

Important variations are evident in this distribution. The high incidence of religion programs in Protestant-related institutions is paralleled by the high proportion with an undergraduate major. In

Table 18

TYPE OF RELIGION PROGRAM BY
INSTITUTIONAL AFFILIATION

	Public	Private Non-Sect.	Roman Catholic	Protestant	Other*
	%	%	%	%	%
Undergraduate Major	35	62	39	81	84
No Major	59	30	44	11	8
No Information on Type	6	8	17	8	8
	100	100	100	100	100
(No. Institutions)	(127)	(103)	(230)	(326)	(26)

*Mostly religiously oriented schools, including Jewish and non-denominational Protestant.

Roman Catholic institutions, however, religion programs have been largely of a service character, often coupled with religion requirements. Only a minority of Roman Catholic institutions offer a religion major, this being a recent innovation for many of them. Undergraduate instruction in religion in the Catholic liberal arts colleges has been offered traditionally to provide basic grounding in religious teaching for the laity. Extended studies in religion and theology were carried on largely in special seminaries directed to the training of clergy and members of the religious orders. Also it was traditionally assumed that philosophical studies might most properly come at the undergraduate level, with theological studies being developed in subsequent education.

Private non-sectarian institutions, in the establishment of religion programs, have moved rapidly to make them parallel to the undergraduate majors offered in other departments, though on the whole the establishment of religion programs in private, non-sectarian schools has come later than in religiously related institutions. Likewise, public institutions have been the most recent to establish religion programs and have thus been still slower in moving to the establishment of a major.

It is evident that the undergraduate major in religion has become an option for undergraduates in every type of institution. Nevertheless, the numbers of undergraduates majoring in religion have been relatively small. Table 19 summarizes information from institutions that offered an undergraduate major in 1970, indicating the numbers of majors graduated in the acaemic years 1963-1964 and 1968-1969. Over half of the institutions in 1968-1969 still graduated seven majors or fewer. Yet the percentage of institutions offering an undergraduate major but not graduating any majors dropped from 32% in 1963-1964 to 12% in 1968-1969, and at the other end of the spectrum, seven percent of the schools graduated 28 or more majors.

Of perhaps greater importance is the fact that the most rapid growth in undergraduate majors has taken place in public and in Roman Catholic institutions. For example, in 1963-64 over half of public institutions with a full program did not graduate any majors in religion, whereas five years later that proportion had dropped to one-fourth. Correlatively, whereas in 1963-1964 only 3% of the public institutions graduated eight or more religion majors, five years later that percentage had increased to 22%. Similarly, in 1963-64, only 24% of the Roman Catholic institutions graduated one or more religion majors and 22% graduated eight or more. (Relatively little change in proportion took place in Protestant or in private non-sectarian institutions, except that in the latter the proportion not graduating any undergraduate religion majors dropped from 27% to 11%.)

The increase in public institutions, is of course, directly related to relatively recent establishment of programs and the rapidly in-

Table 19

UNDERGRADUATE DEGREES WITH MAJORS IN RELIGION

Number of Majors Graduated	Percent of Institutions 1963-64	1968-69
	%	%
None	32	12
1-3	21	29
4-7	21	24
8-11	12	14
12-15	5	5
16-19	2	5
20-23	2	2
24-27	1	2
28 or more	4	7
	100	100
(No. of Institutions reporting)	(346)	(353)

creasing registrations in religion. The sharp increase in Roman Catholic colleges, in spite of the decline in religion course enrollments, noted earlier, reflects the transformation of undergraduate religion departments. General service programs in Catholic schools, with several courses required of all or many students, often with no undergraduate major offered, have been changed into elective programs parallel to other departments and majors. Yet it remains true that in all types of institutions, religion departments tend to be service departments, with the bulk of their enrollments coming in a few courses from students who take an elective or two out of general interest.

There is relatively little variation among institutions in the total number of courses required for the undergraduate major. About three-fifths of the schools require between six and eleven courses, although nearly a fourth of the institutions report requiring eighteen or more courses. (These variations are also related to differing patterns of academic bookkeeping—e.g., course units versus semester credits, and three-credit versus two-credit courses. Thus the gross figures tell us very little about programs.) Roman Catholic and conservative Protestant institutions tend to require more courses for the major than do the other types of schools.

Of greater importance, both in relation to the undergraduate major and the general service character of most religion departments, is the extent to which religion courses have specific course prerequisites. Thirty percent of the reporting institutions indicate that they had no courses with religion prerequisites; twenty-one percent had prerequisites for fewer than 20% of their courses;

twenty-seven percent had prerequisites for 20% to 47% of their offerings; and the remaining twenty-two percent of the departments had prerequisites for over 47% of all courses which they offered.

    c. Patterns of course offerings. Most revealing about the actual undergraduate religion curricula is the distribution of course offerings. Table 20 summarizes data from 358 institutions with a full

Table 20

TYPES OF UNDERGRADUATE RELIGION COURSES OFFERED*

Course Area or Title	Total No. courses offered	Percent of institutions offering one or more courses in the area			
		Public (N=36)	Private Non-sect. (N=61)	Roman Catholic (N=66)	Protestant (N=195)
		%	%	%	%
Introduction to Religion	360	61	39	36	38
Old Testament or New Testament	1,368	72	85	74	76
History of Christianity or Christian Thought	531	33	49	36	78
Systematic Theology	307	29	26	51	31
Roman Catholicism	157	18	20	52	33
Protestantism	67	8	5	40	5
Eastern Orthodoxy	20	6	2	11	1
Judaism	146	39	30	30	16
Ethics	332	58	44	62	54
Contemporary Religious Problems/Thought	369	64	46	42	51
Philosophy of Religion	176	47	44	23	42
World Religions/History of Religions	279	45	49	35	61
Religions of the East (combined)	101	42	21	18	15
A Specific Eastern Religion	143	36	21	8	5
Islam	30	18	11	5	4
Primitive Religion	48	14	5	17	6
Religion and Society	83	30	11	12	14
Sociology of Religion	53	22	11	11	8
Psychology of Religion	74	25	13	15	17
Religion in America	179	42	46	23	34
Afro-American/Black Religion	34	8	10	6	6
Religion and Culture	90	39	15	11	13
Religion and Literature	81	36	16	18	14

*Based on reports from 358 institutions. Each institution was asked to report how many courses were offered in 1969-1970 in each of the specified areas, counting each course only once, and assigning it to the area most appropriate. The column "Total No. courses offered" gives the combined total for all the schools. The percent columns show what percent of institutions offered <u>one or more</u> courses of the types specified. Thirty-three institutions of various other religious affiliations have not been included in this tabulation.

program—indicating the total number of courses in each area offered by the whole group of institutions, plus the percentage of institutions of each type offering at least one course in the areas designated.

In general Table 20 shows the continuing heavy concentration on Christian studies in the undergraduate curriculum. It is only the courses in the Christian area that are likely to be found in more than 50% of the schools. (Yet it is also noteworthy how many types of courses appear in fewer than a third of the schools.) Old Testament and New Testament are the most widely represented courses in every type of institution, including public colleges. This category includes specialized courses within the Old and New Testament, hence the large total number of courses offered, but it does not include general introductions to Bible, which are offered in some institutions, though in considerably fewer than those that offer Old and New Testament separately. The focus on Christian studies may also be partly reflected in the high percentages of schools offering courses in ethics and in contemporary religious problems or religious thought—though in both instances there is also evidence of a growing interest in problem oriented courses. The history of Christian thought is widely represented in private non-sectarian as well as in church-related institutions.

The study of non-Western religions is obviously most commonly found in the form of a single course in world religions. Relatively little is offered in specialized and presumably advanced courses in the religions of the East, either as a whole or individually, e.g., Hinduism, Buddhism, or Chinese and Japanese religions. Except for public institutions, only a fifth or fewer of the schools offered courses devoted specifically to the religions of the East.

Studies in Judaism are moderately represented, except in Protestant institutions. It is astonishing, however, that so little is done with Islam (or, within the Christian orbit, with Eastern Orthodoxy).

Courses in the development of religion in America have made their way significantly though more slowly in Protestant institutions and still more slowly in Roman Catholic schools. The study of Afro-American or Black religion has only begun to appear.

Public institutions are shown in Table 20 to have markedly different curricula from the other types of schools. These universities and colleges have most extensively devised specific courses called Introduction to Religion. They are likely to offer courses in Judaism as in the history of Christianity or Christian thought (though the systematic study of Christian theology is also significantly represented in these institutions). It is in the public sector, furthermore, that the study of Eastern religions, both by courses covering the Eastern traditions as a whole and by specific courses in those traditions, is most widely represented. Public institutions are twice as likely as the other type of schools to have courses in religion and society, in sociology of religion, in religion and culture, and in religion and literature. They also appear to have more highly developed curricula in the psychology of religion.

Private non-sectarian institutions are distinctive in curricula in that they have the highest proportion of schools offering courses in Old Testament or New Testament, that they are much more likely than Roman Catholic or Protestant schools to offer courses in one or another of the specific Eastern religions (though only a fifth of the private institutions do this), and that they are on a par with public institutions in the study of religion in America. The incidence of courses in ethics is somewhat lower than in the other types of schools.

Roman Catholic schools are distinctive in the extent to which courses are offered in systematic theology, in Roman Catholicism, and in Protestantism (the latter being an emphasis growing especially out of the ecumenical movement in the 1960's). The percentage of Roman Catholic schools offering courses in the history of Christianity or in Christian thought appears to be low (36%), but this is counterbalanced by the high incidence of courses in Roman Catholicism and in Protestantism. Similarly, the relatively low frequency of philosophy of religion courses is counterbalanced by the higher proportion of systematic or dogmatic theological studies. The study of non-Western religions has made its way much more slowly in Roman Catholic schools, with only 35% having even introduced a survey course in world religions.

Protestant institutions have by far the highest incidence of courses in the history of Christianity or of Christian thought. They offer courses in Roman Catholicism more frequently than either public or private non-sectarian schools. The Protestant institutions also have the highest incidence of courses in the specific traditions of the East or even of the Eastern religions as such.

The summary in Table 20 is also striking in showing what is not being done. Conclusions must be drawn carefully, since course areas overlap (e.g., ethics, contemporary religious problems, and philosophy of religion; as well as religion and society with sociology of religion). But it is noteworthy that the great majority of institutions offer no courses at all in religion and society, sociology of religion, or psychology of religion, at least within their religion programs. Only a minority of institutions have attempted to devise a special introduction to religion. And as we have noted, Islam, primitive religions and Eastern Orthodoxy get very short shrift.

d. Faculty fields. The curricular patterns indicated by the distribution of course offerings is paralleled by the distribution of undergraduate faculty specializations, indicated in Table 21. Two questions were asked in eliciting this information: what is the present primary area of specialization, and what was the field of graduate training of each member of the faculty? One choice was to be made in each case from a list of 33 fields. The list was deliberately skewed towards much finer distinctions within the areas of Christian studies, since it was plain that the majority of faculty would be included here. In Table 21, the fields are listed in rank order of the present primary areas of specialization.

Table 21

FIELDS OF SPECIALIZATION OF RELIGION FACULTY

	Present Specialization		Primary Area of Graduate Training	
	No.	%	No.	%
Systematic Theology/Dogmatic Theology	476	13.0	612	17.7
New Testament	475	13.0	436	12.6
Old Testament	328	9.0	251	7.2
Ethics/Moral Theology/Social Ethics	298	8.1	192	5.6
History of Christian Thought/ Theology	246	6.7	279	8.1
History of Christianity/Church History	191	5.2	200	5.8
Philosophy of Religion	190	5.2	172	5.0
History of Religions/Comparative Religion/Phenomenology of Religion	168	4.6	95	2.7
Religious Education	159	4.3	180	5.2
Philosophy	141	3.8	163	4.7
Judaica/Jewish History/Hebraic Studies	131	3.6	110	3.2
Religion & Literature/Theology & Culture	103	2.8	56	1.6
Religions of the East	72	2.0	53	1.0
Religion in America	72	2.0	53	1.0
Pastoral Theology/Homiletics	64	1.7	67	1.9
Sociology of Religion	57	1.6	41	1.2
Psychology of Religion	52	1.4	46	1.3
Ancient Near Eastern Religion	41	1.1	40	1.2
Liturgy	38	1.0	31	0.9
History	32	0.9	61	1.8
Literature	25	0.7	28	0.8
Sociology	22	0.6	26	0.8
Buddhism	22	0.6	14	0.4
Hinduism	21	0.6	17	0.5
Islam	18	0.5	13	0.4
Chinese Religion	14	0.4	10	0.3
Linguistics	14	0.4	18	0.5
Psychology	14	0.4	30	0.9
Education	13	0.4	44	1.3
Classics	12	0.3	21	0.6
Anthropology	11	0.3	11	0.3
Primitive Religion	7	0.2	2	0.0
Other	134	3.7	110	3.2
	3,662	100.1	3,462	100.2

It is evident from this distribution that the faculty resources are massively concentrated in the area of Christian studies, particularly theology and the history of Christian thought, the history of Christianity, biblical studies, and ethics. Furthermore, the relative concentrations in the several fields have not changed much between the graduate specializations and the present primary fields of activity. Equally important, however, are some noteworthy gains and losses in particular fields and changes between faculty members' areas of graduate training and present specializations.

A further analysis of the data from which this table is drawn shows that for the most part individuals have continued to work primarily within their fields of graduate specialization. Specifically, in most of the fields cited, between 75% and 85% of the persons trained in the field are now specializing in it. Major exceptions, however, are found in the following fields: systematic theology, with only 63% of those with graduate specialization in this area being still considered as concentrating in it; the history of Christian thought, also with 63%; religion and literature and/or theology of culture, with only 55%; and pastoral theology, with 60%.

In systematic or dogmatic theology there has been a large net loss: of 612 persons trained in the field, only 387 are identified as still specializing in it. These faculty have moved into a variety of areas, notably into ethics, but also significantly into theology and literature, biblical studies, history of Christian thought, and history of religions. The movement into theology from other areas has been small.

The most volatile field has been religion and literature and/or theology of culture—admittedly a loosely defined area. As we noted, only 55% of the persons with this as their primary graduate training field are still concentrating mainly in it, yet the area has had a relatively large gain in personnel. The consequence is that only a third of those now working primarily in the field have this identified as their area of graduate specialization.

Along with religion and literature, the fields with the largest gains, relative to the numbers with graduate specialization in the field, are: history of religions, religions of the East, and ethics. Of these, only in ethics can more than half of the present faculty be identified with graduate specialization in the same field.

We have from this study no information on the extent to which faculty transferring into new areas have received postgraduate training in them, though we know that in many instances this is the case. Nor is the total extent of change in areas of specialization necessarily large. We probably have here one symbol of the frequent requirement on religion teachers, particularly in small departments, to work in areas beyond those in which they specifically trained. More significant, we have a clear indication of the growing importance, on the one hand, of the history of religions and the religions of the East, and on the other hand, of ethics and "religion and culture."

We also see in the spectrum of specializations those areas that are relatively weak in faculty resources. These are confirmed by reports from department chairmen concerning their priorities for new faculty appointments. The top priorities went by far to new appointments in the area of history of religions or comparative religions. Relative to the present numbers of faculty in the field, the religions of the East, Islam and religion and literature/theology and culture claimed very high place. Substantial numbers of chairmen also gave priorities to faculty in the traditional fields—biblical studies, history of Christianity and Christian thought, philosophy and ethics—but these ranked much lower in proportion to the present numbers of faculty in those areas.[12]

6. The Study of Religion in Two-Year Colleges[13]

a. The incidence of religion offerings in the several types of two-year institutions is indicated by Table 22, reporting the numbers and proportions of institutions of each type offering religion courses.

Subject to the qualifications noted in Footnote 13 it appears that nearly all Protestant and Roman Catholic two-year institutions offer courses in religion, as do half of the private non-sectarian institutions. Since public institutions constitute by far the largest group of two-year colleges, it is of special importance to note that approximately two-fifths (42%) of the public schools have religion courses. The pattern may be compared with the proportions of four-year institutions offering academic study in religion. Among four-year institutions, the percentages in Protestant and Roman Catholic schools are precisely the same as those reported for two-year colleges. In four-year public institutions, however, 51% reported offering religion courses, and in private non-sectarian colleges 63% offered religion courses.

Table 22

TWO-YEAR COLLEGES OFFERING RELIGION COURSES,
1970-1971
by institutional affiliation

	Number of Respondents	Number offering Religion Courses	Percentage of Respondents Offering Religion Courses
Public	232	97	42%
Private	40	20	50%
Protestant	46	45	98%
Catholic	20	20	100%

b. Except in the church-related schools it is not really appropriate to speak of religion "curricula" because of the small numbers of course offerings, in comparison with four-year colleges. The average public two-year college offering religion courses in the academic year 1970-1971 reported slightly less than two such courses. The typical private institution offered slightly less than three courses. Protestant and Roman Catholic institutions, on the other hand, offered slightly more than five courses and four courses respectively.

If we ask what *kinds* of courses are offered, the answer is that the areas emphasized are generally parallel to those in four-year colleges, with the major exceptions of theology and the history of Christianity. Tables 23 and 24 show the patterns of concentration in broad course areas, with respect both to the proportions of types of schools offering any courses in the fields listed and to the distribution of the total number of courses offered in each type of institution. In these classifications "Bible" includes both introduction to Bible and specialized courses in the Jewish and Christian scriptures. "Christianity" includes introduction to Christianity as well as courses in the history of Christianity and Christian thought. "Contemporary beliefs" includes a variety of courses dealing with contemporary problems, issues or theology. Interestingly, courses specifically in Judaism or in the history of Western religious thought as distinguished from Christianity, were so few in number as not to be worth tabulating. The principal kinds of courses here classified as "other" were scattered among a number of areas, including principally ethics, "marriage," biblical languages (Greek), religious education, psychology of religion, and practical theology (e.g., homiletics, missions).

Obviously, the courses offered in two-year colleges tend to

Table 23

PERCENT OF INSTITUTIONS OFFERING ONE OR MORE RELIGION COURSES IN VARIOUS FIELDS
by institutional affiliation
182 Two-Year Colleges, 1970-1971

	Public	Private	Protestant	Catholic
	%	%	%	%
Introduction to Religion	5	10	7	10
Bible	52	70	98	75
Christianity	1	5	38	30
World Religions	53	55	27	25
Contemporary Beliefs	15	20	20	80
Other	8	25	44	65
	(N=97)	(N=20)	(N=45)	(N=20)

Table 24

DISTRIBUTION OF TOTAL RELIGION COURSES,
by fields and institutional affiliation,
182 Two-Year Colleges, 1970-1971

	Public	Private	Protestant	Catholic
	%	%	%	%
Introduction to Religion	3	3	1	2
Bible	53	46	60	31
Christianity	0	0	10	10
World Religions	30	30	5	6
Contemporary Beliefs	6	10	4	34
Other	8	10	20	17
	100	100	100	100
	(N=186)	(N=61)	(N=232)	(N=88)

cluster heavily in a few areas: Bible, in all types of schools; world religions, in public and private non-sectarian schools; and contemporary beliefs (or theology) in Catholic schools. These are the areas most likely to be represented even when only two or three courses are offered.

Bible courses constitute more than half of all courses given in the 182 institutions (Table 24). Public and private non-sectarian institutions (which offer the smallest numbers of courses per school) are most likely to offer Bible (frequently under the title Bible as Literature) and World Religions (Table 23). Surprisingly, not only do half the public two-year colleges offer at least one course in Bible; over half of the total religion courses in the public schools are in Bible (Table 24), as compared with 30% in the area of world religions. Nearly all Protestant schools (98%) offer Bible, though the total proportion of Bible courses is less (60%), partly because of the larger average number of courses offered. In Roman Catholic schools, while most (75%) teach Bible, the proportion of Bible courses is much lower (31%) — a greater weight falling on courses in theology, philosophy of religion and ethics.

The study of world religion is very sparsely represented in church-related two-year colleges. It is further evident from both Table 23 and Table 24 that very few two-year institutions have undertaken to develop special introductions to the study of religion. Rather it is most frequently courses in Bible that serve this purpose, followed in the case of public and private institutions by courses in world religions.

c. It is a corollary of the small numbers of religion courses offered in two-year colleges that few faculty are involved. In the institutions offering courses in religion from which reports are available, the average public institution had 1.3 total faculty teaching religion in 1970-71, the typical private institution 1.5 faculty, and the typical Protestant and Roman Catholic institutions had 2.6 and 2.3 respectively. Equally important, however, religion instruction in two-year colleges has been overwhelmingly offered by part-time faculty, i.e., either part-time faculty members in the institution or full-time faculty who divide their teaching responsibility with some other area. Table 25 shows the distribution of faculty by full-time/part-time status in the several kinds of institutions.

Of 313 total faculty in 1970-1971, 108 were part-time faculty and 138 were full-time teachers combining their work in religion with one or more other fields, notably philosophy, literature, sociology, and history. The highest percentage of full-time religion faculty is found in Protestant schools (43%). In public junior colleges, however, out of 129 faculty teaching religion in 1970-71 only three were full-time in religion. In all types of institutions, except Roman Catholic, a large proportion of the total faculty were full-time teachers but also taught in other areas. About half of these were reported as having their primary specialization in the other fields.

It is also significant that both Roman Catholic and public institutions relied heavily on the use of part-time faculty, private institutions somewhat less so and Protestant schools least.[14] This usually means the use of local clergy and/or chaplains. (It is surprising that this pattern is least common in Protestant institutions.)

d. What generalizations can be drawn from these summaries and from the further comments offered by junior college administrators? First of all, it is obvious that the patterns of the academic study of religion in two-year institutions generally follow those of the four-year colleges, though in the former the curricula are much more modest and less multifaceted. Academic courses in religion

Table 25

DISTRIBUTION OF FACULTY BY FULL AND PART-TIME STATUS
182 Two-year Colleges, 1970-1971

	Public	Private	Protestant	Catholic
	%	%	%	%
Full-time instruction in Religion	2	27	43	24
Full-time faculty but teaching in some other area as well as rel.	55	40	40	26
Part-time faculty	43	33	17	50
Total	100	100	100	100
	(N=129)	(N=29)	(N=110)	(N=45)

are somewhat less widespread among public and private two-year colleges than in their four-year counterparts, but this will also be true of many other curricular areas with the exception of such universally present fields as English, history, natural science, and the like. Since many junior colleges, particularly those which emphasize the liberal arts, are "feeder" institutions for state and local universities, they face the problem of ordering their curricula to the average requirements for freshmen and sophomores in such four-year institutions. At this primary level, religion courses may receive a low "elective" priority, since students must first fulfill requirements for transfer to four-year institutions. Further in numerous instances, regulations of public institutions do not provide for the transfer of credit for courses in religion.

The study of religion in two-year institutions inevitably remains largely at the introductory level. Rarely, however, are there attempts to devise special courses in the introduction to religion. Rather the pattern is to offer introductory level courses in the several areas, notably Bible and world religions (the latter in the case of public and private institutions). Introductions to Christianity or to theology assume a prominent role in church-related institutions. Protestant institutions in particular tend to order their curricula around Bible courses. Catholic institutions generally find in "theology" the focal point of the curriculum—though this involves a certain flexibility, since theology is often expanded to include ethics, philosophy, and contemporary religious problems. The absence of specific introductions to religion may also be correlated with the difficulty of integrating such courses into curricular patterns concentrating on other areas.

The most serious problem for two-year institutions appears to be that of faculty resources, specifically the need to rely on part-time faculty, either those who are only part-time instructors or those who share teaching responsibility in another area. As already noted, a large proportion of the faculty fall into the latter category. Some of these have had their primary training in religion or are now specializing in religion. Equally often, these are faculty trained and working mainly in literature, philosophy or the social sciences, to whom responsibilities for teaching in religion have been given. There are natural associations, but the student encountering college study of religion for the first time may be seriously handicapped by the lack of advanced study in the field by their instructors. In a few instances, this practical necessity of joint responsibility has been made a virtue by the development of interdisciplinary courses per se. One junior college, for example, has erected a liberal arts (humanities) program using Bible as a main theme. But there is little evidence to show that deliberate or structured interdisciplinary studies have become widespread.

Only a few institutions not now offering courses in religion indicated their intention to enter the field. In general, however, among those institutions offering religion courses, there was a widespread desire to expand, largely because of student interest as gauged by enrollment in already existing courses or because of the desire to extend the variety of course offerings. Reasons given for not starting or expanding religion programs included mainly low budget priorities, lack of available faculty, the problem of transfer of credit for religion courses to four-year institutions, and the lack of overall facilities due to the newness of the institution, etc. The major areas accounted desirable for expansion include comparative religious studies, Asian studies (and in public institutions particularly, Western religions). Biblical studies are accounted an area of needed growth particularly in the non-Protestant schools ("Biblical studies" here includes the Bible as literature, the history of Old Testament religion, Bible and contemporary issues, and studies in primitive Christianity). Numerous institutions expressed a desire to include courses in the philosophy of religion, which was taken in several instances to include comparative religions, or contemporary religious problems, or methodology for religious study. Contemporary issues in religion (including presumably current theology, religion and science and assorted ethical issues) was frequently noted as a desideratum, and a few institutions hoped to include courses in religion in America, religion and culture, and the like. In sum, the goals for expansion in two-year institutions appear largely to parallel those of four-year colleges. There is little evidence, however, that development is likely to occur by the appointment of full-time religion faculty or by the incorporation of elaborate distinct religion curricula. The combination of religion and other fields will continue to be a dominant pattern — and this presents both difficulties and opportunities. The difficulties will arise especially in the finding of adequately trained faculty (e.g., those who can treat Asian religions at more than a patently superficial and misleading level). The opportunities will grow from the freedom of limitation by traditional patterns of emphasis and the resultant possibility of experimentation with interdisciplinary and cross-disciplinary studies. These opportunities have so far rarely been seized, but they lie close at hand.

[1]This account is based largely on data collected as a part of the Study of Graduate Education in Religion, sponsored by the American Council of Learned Societies, with a grant from the Henry Luce Foundation, Inc., a study conducted during 1969-71 under the direction of the editor of the present volume. As background for the analysis of graduate studies, an attempt was made to secure information concerning as many as possible of the presently existing undergraduate religion programs. The director was assisted in the latter task by the Center for Research on the Acts of Man, directed by Professor Samuel Z. Klausner of the Department of Sociology of the University of Pennsylvania. From responses to a simple screening questionnaire, sent in the Winter of 1969-1970 to the heads of 2,335 institutions, a list of 1,311 four-year accredited colleges in the United States and Canada was compiled. (Of the original list of institutions, 1,024 were eliminated as not being four-year institutions.) Of the 1,311 four-year colleges, 873 claimed to have a special program or department of religion and to them was sent a detailed questionnaire in March 1970. By May 4, 1970, 592 questionnaires (68%) had been returned and this date was

taken as the cut-off point for initial computer processing. Of these responses, 404 indicated an undergraduate major or combined major in religion, whereas 188 reported that no major in religion was offered. Detailed studies, bearing particularly on structure and curriculum, were made of the 404 "full programs." Further tabulations included both the full and partial programs. Eventually, 644 responses (75%) to the questionnaire were received and a number of studies, particularly relating to faculty characteristics, were made of this whole group. In addition, 114 replies were received to a brief follow-up questionnaire sent in the Fall of 1970 to all those who did not return the main questionnaire; thus certain items of summary information are available for a total of 768 (88%) undergraduate institutions with religion programs.

The results of that survey have been published in part in Chapter 9 of the study report: Graduate Education in Religion: A Critical Appraisal, by Claude Welch, University of Montana Press (1971), copies of which are available from the Council on the Study of Religion. The reader is referred to that volume for more detailed exhibition of the data discussed in some of the following sections, particularly Sections 1 and 2, as well as for a more detailed statement of the survey procedures and for a complete list of the undergraduate institutions surveyed. Material from that report is used by permission.

For the present discussion, further studies have been made of the data in hand and a number of items have been incorporated which could not for reasons of space be included in the report of the ACLS study. A few slight variations in numbers and percentages, between the present summary and the corresponding discussions in the earlier report, are the result of the addition of further data.

In addition, during the Summer of 1971, a survey was made of religion offerings in two-year colleges, as a basis for the discussion in Section 6 below.

[2]Associate Justice Clark, in the majority opinion in that case, wrote: ... It might well be said that one's education is not complete without a study of comparative religion or the history of religion and its relationship to the advancement of civilization. It certainly may be said that the Bible is worthy of study for its literary and historical qualities. Nothing we have said here indicates that such study of the Bible or of religion, when presented objectively as part of a secular program of education, may not be effected consistent with the First Amendment. (Abingdon School District versus Schempp, 374 U.S. 203, 225 (1963).

It seems that, at least with respect to the United States Constitution, the question of the legality of the study of religion is no longer in doubt. The distinction between "study about religion" and "instruction in religion," though that phraseology is not altogether happy and may often be misleading, is frequently used to suggest the distinction between what the Supreme Court approved and the kind of religious instruction that is intended directly to serve the interests of a religious community.

[3]The comparison here between religion course registrants and total undergraduate enrollments may involve some distortion, particularly in the case of the church-related institutions, since some students would have been enrolled for more than one course. But the basic pattern of differences will not be altered.

[4]James Cass and Max Birnbaum, Comparative Guide to American Colleges, 1969: George Nash, "A Description of the 1,444 Accredited Four-Year Institutions of Higher Education," Bureau of Applied Social Research, Columbia University, unpublished report, 1969. Fuller details of these indices and the correlations with religion programs are to be found in Graduate Education in Religion: A Critical Appraisal, Chapter 9.

[5]The basic pattern of change can be seen in a highly compressed way also in the development of a religion program in a state university, the University of North Carolina, as described in Robert Spivey, "Modest Messiahs: The Study of Religion in State Universities," Religious Education, LXIII (1969), 5-12. The department was established in 1946 as a result of the generosity of a donor who wanted the Bible studied as part of the University's curriculum. The aim was plainly that of "bringing faith and morality to the secular campus, ... teaching the Bible in order for students to be morally and spiritually uplifted." Thus the first chair was a professorship of Bible. A second purpose which emerged was that of "opening a dialogue between religion and other academic areas in order to uncover their 'presuppositions' so that the Judeo-Christian world view might compete within the university as the integrative perspective from which to view other disciplines." Throughout the 1950's and early 60's these purposes dominated the work of the department, and it remained basically a "service" department. Beginning in the mid 1960's, however, the purposes of more empirical examination of religious phenomena, with a movement outward toward other academic areas, including sociology, psychology, art and literature, came to provide the basic focus for the work of the department and this shift was paralleled by a remarkable expansion in undergraduate enrollments and faculty.

[6]Note that the relative emphases of the programs classified as "other" follow closely the patterns of conservative Protestant and Roman Catholic institutions. This is explained by the fact

that the category "other" comprises largely institutions of Jewish or non-denomination conservative Protestant orientation.

[7]Outside budgetary support for departments of religion appears to be rare. Ninety-three percent of the institutions reporting indicated that their religion programs were funded entirely from the parent institution, either as a distinct budgetary unit or in combination with another department or in the central college budget. Only one percent explicitly indicated that support was received from outside church sources as well as from the parent institution.

[8]For information concerning faculty ordination, age, and earned degrees (including sources of highest degrees), see Graduate Education in Religion: A Critical Appraisal, Chapter 9.

[9]With the exception of Protestant schools in the 509-1,020 religion enrollment range.

[10]Oddly, a few of the institutions offering an undergraduate major (3%) reported that no credit is allowed toward graduation for religion courses and another 4% indicated that not more than six religion courses could be counted toward graduation. One suspects some errors in reporting here.

[11]I am here extrapolating (a) from the fact that of the 768 schools from which we have definite information concerning the type of religion program, 532 offer an undergraduate major, and (b) from evidence that the general character of the other (105) institutions identified as having a religion program is like that of the 768.

[12]These conclusions are based on responses from 332 departmental chairmen to questions asking for their first, second, and third priorities for forthcoming appointments, either for expansion or for replacement. (See Graduate Education in Religion: A Critical Appraisal, Table 9-18)

[13]In June and July 1971, a brief questionnaire was sent to 527 two-year institutions asking for the following kinds of curricular information: Were religion courses offered in the academic year 1970-1971, and if so, what courses? If not, is it planned that such courses will be offered in the near future? Are there plans for expansion either in the numbers of courses or by the introduction of new areas of study? Information requested concerning faculty included: academic rank, primary field of specialization, full or part-time status in the institution, other fields of teaching responsibility.

The questionnaires were sent to a random sample made up of one-third of 1,076 junior colleges listed in Patterson's Guide to American Education (editor Noman Elliott, Vol. LXVII, Educational Directories, Mt. Prospect, Illinois, 1971), plus approximately 200 other institutions on the list, which on the basis of earlier study were known to have offerings or programs in the field of religion. Responses were received from 338 institutions (64% of the questionnaires distributed). The distribution of responses in relation to institutional affiliation roughly approximates the nationwide distribution of schools. The Patterson guide list does not provide full information concerning religious affiliation. However, the Education Directory: Higher Education 1970-71 (HEW, U.S. G.P.O. 1971) provides data on 897 two-year institutions by religious affiliation. The following tabulation shows the distribution of institutions in that list, compared with the distribution of respondents to the questionnaire. Except for Protestant schools, the distribution of responses is generally parallel to the national pattern. The bias in the sample, introduced by the inclusion of a large number of institutions already known to have religion offerings, thus results in a much higher proportion of the Protestant institutions in the survey. Roman Catholic schools may be slightly overrepresented. Public institutions are slightly underrepresented. Conclusions should not be drawn from this survey, therefore, concerning the total proportion of two-year institutions offering religious studies. Reliable conclusions can be drawn, however, concerning the relative incidence of religion offerings within each of the types of institution, and in particular concerning the kinds of curricula involved. These were our special interest in the survey.

	National Distribution	Distribution Of Responses
	%	%
Public	73	68
Private	13	12
Protestant	8	14
Catholic	5	6
	99	100
	(N=897)	(N=338)

[14]A Texas junior college offers a useful illustration of a pattern still common in some areas, namely, of the offering of religion courses by faculty externally supported on various "bible chairs." The 1971-1972 annual catalog lists a total of eight courses under the section on Bible, six of which are introductory courses in Bible, one an introduction to Christianity and one selected studies in church history. The courses are "given by affiliation with the Baptist chair of Bible, the Bible chair of Texas Methodist student movement, the Fifth Street Presbyterian Bible chair, and the Church of Christ Bible chair." Up to 12 semester hours are accepted for degree credit; however, the institution indicates that it does not itself offer courses in religion, nor is it planning to do so in the future. None of the Bible courses is listed in any of the suggested degree programs.

Part III
Innovation and
Experiment: Samplings

Innovation and
Experiment: Samplings

Introduction

In sharp contrast to the schematic and heavily statistical summaries in Part II, our interest now is mainly in the unusual, in diversity and experiment. There we sought a fixed and reliable cross-section; here the focus is blurred by the motion of the object. There our interest was in completeness of data and representative generalization; here we have drawn a quite irregular kind of sample. A fairly wide net has been cast in the attempt to discover the new and distinctive ventures, and in this way to expose the issues. But it is obvious that this net will have missed at least as many interesting and valuable experiments as it has captured. Furthermore, the choices made from the mass of material at hand inevitably involve highly subjective decisions as to what constitutes innovation.

The questions about directions of change, novelty, and experiment, have been organized into several broad groups: (1) What are the patterns of introduction to the study of religion? (2) What are the varying styles of undergraduate religion curricula as a whole? (3) What is the role and definition of the undergraduate major? (4) What are the directions of inter-disciplinary and cross-disciplinary study? (5) What are the kinds of experimentation in course and procedures as well as subject matter? These areas inevitably overlap.

In the following descriptions we have deliberately emphasized the contrasts and the variants, because the goal is not to foreclose options for the future or to specify *the* right directions of development. Significant broad tendencies do emerge and some of these we may believe need to be encouraged. But it would be unfortunate if the net result of our interpretation were simply to support a move toward uniformity or to encourage conformity to a single model for undergraduate religion programs.

The interpretations draw heavily on descriptions and reflections provided by department chairmen and the designers of individual courses. In most cases the language is our own, though it is always based on quite specific descriptions and reports. All the illustrations referred to here come from the period 1969-71. It goes without saying that these are illustrations plucked from mid-stream, and just because they are innovative and experimental they may be expected to have already been modified. Yet, their value as illustrations is not diminished. The emphasis therefore is on specific instances, including brief case studies. Enough connecting tissue is provided to identify common and emerging issues, which are then drawn together briefly at the end.

1. Where to Begin? - The Introduction to Religion

Two distinct but related questions are involved in the problem of beginnings: what is the proper basis for further study and what should be proposed for the student who elects only a course or two in the field? With few exceptions, the traditional answers to both these questions fall into three categories. First, and most widely, it has been judged that the natural place to begin is the Bible, i.e., either in a general introduction to Biblical literature or in separate courses in Old Testament and New Testament. This has been most characteristic, of course, of Protestant institutions because of the emphasis on scriptural authority. Where religion courses have been required, again particularly in Protestant institutions, it is most commonly biblical courses that have been involved. But quite apart from the interests of the religious communities, it can be argued that because of the great importance of biblical literature for the whole of Western culture, nothing is more natural and important than to have a thorough grounding in the content and interpretation of Scripture. Thus even in public institutions, Bible courses have occupied a large place among introductory courses.

The second traditional pattern is the "world religions" course or sequence, on the assumption that the *sine qua non* for the study of religion is a cognizance of the great religious traditions. This style of approach is exemplified not only by the common two-term sequence, "Religions of the East" and "Religions of the West" (Judaism, Christianity and Islam), but also by the many undergraduate courses in the dominant traditions in America (Judaism, Catholicism, Protestantism), and in public institutions it has been especially prominent.

The third most common approach has been the introductory philosophy of religion or the introduction to theology—the latter mainly in Roman Catholic schools.

In describing these three approaches as traditional, we do not mean to suggest that they are illegitimate or outworn, or that they have vanished from the scene. The former hegemony of biblical studies is being challenged, but all three of these patterns of introductory study are widespread in all types of schools (including two-year institutions) and strong arguments can be given for their validity. Yet several other patterns of introduction have begun to come to the fore, posing more self-consciously the question of beginnings. Among them are some of the most interesting experiments.

In the emergence of these recent patterns, certain issues recur. Is the dominant task to be one of organizing information concerning religious phenomena and history, or one of engaging the student's interests, though in a non-authoritarian way, in questions of truth and value that arise in the religious traditions? How is one to relate the responsibility for studying the major religions in their historical development and inner coherence, i.e., as entities, to the desirability of exhibiting the manifold roles of "the religious" in cultural life generally. Neither of these issues is properly put as the question of "objectivity" versus existential relevance, for it is agreed that "objectivity and relevance are false alternatives; what really counts is a passion for inquiry." Objectivity is not the absence of passion but a particular kind of passion, and the deepest kind of relevance emerges only as the passion for inquiry is released and supported.

Some of the recent approaches to the introduction to religion also reflect not only the common service course function of religion courses, i.e., the fact that most students will participate in only one or two religion courses, but also the recognition that introductory study in religion may frequently serve as the first or primary introduction to the humanities at the college level. Thus the emphasis may be less on a comprehensive body of knowledge than on processes of inquiry. It is to be doubted whether the study of religion has unique problems at this point. Religion is plainly not like physics or chemistry in being susceptible to vertical structuring in which each level builds on clearly definable preceding stages. More like history and English, it may have multiple points of entry in subject matter. But at the same time, religion now has the peculiar problem of rarely being able to presuppose prior academic study in the field.[1] The severity of this difficulty is even greater than, e.g., in sociology and psychology. The newer patterns of introduction to religion also share in one way or another the question of defining the identity and character of the subject matter religion. The context for this problem is not the framework of a single religious tradition, whose teaching and history can be broken down into manageable units. Nor is it even the generally recognized major religious traditions as such. Rather the question becomes, what are the demarcations of religious phenomena? Is there a *homo religiosus*, an identifiable "religious experience," or something called "the sacred" or "the holy" which qualifies an experience as religious? Or, since religions differ not only in the answers they given to questions but in the formulation of questions, differing even over what are the significant issues for mankind, is the task of an introduction to religion, as many would have it "a cumulative inquiry into a variety of ways in which religious issues come to be defined, religious questions come to be raised, religious proposals become articulated, and religious alternatives take shape." A primary task therefore is that of disabusing students of their perhaps inadequate and misleading "preunderstandings" about religion.

These issues are further complicated by the recognition that religion has to do not only with concepts and belief systems but with images and symbols expressed in forms of art and architecture, literature, music, and dance. Religious behavior involves personal and corporate patterns of enactment, affective as well as cognitive dimensions of existence. All religious rhythms and styles, moreover, take place in the context of particular cultural possibilities and resources.[2]

The permutations of such considerations may be illustrated by several specific, recently devised introductions to religion. Because they share many of the same concerns, those experiments do not fall into easily separable types. All use cross-cultural examples, all have a stake in the methodological question, all have an interest in contemporary religious expression and possibilities. Many use novels and other non-traditional materials and explicitly seek to enlarge the concept of the religious. Many eschew the scheme of chronological development as an organizing form. But differences in emphasis, as well as in style, suggest the presence of at least three or four distinguishable tendencies.

For example, Western Michigan's Introduction to Religion plainly belongs to a pattern in which the dominant concern is with the *method* for studying religion, and in this case, with the exploration of a distinctive methodology for studying religion "as a generic mode of human experience." The data are to be structured and interpreted "in terms of an autonomous discipline which is specifically designed to consider the nature and history of man's encounter with the Sacred." This is no narrowly conceived approach, for the data are identified as coming from many sources, including the disciplines of anthropology, archaeology, sociology, psychology, history, philosophy, and the arts. Hence the approach to religion must include (1) "the historical problem," recognizing that religion occurs in history and that historical connection and change must be interpreted, (2) "the morphological problem," particularly the relation of religious forms to each other and to other modes of human expression, (3) "the constructive problems," particularly the application of discoveries about religion to existential questions, i.e., one's perception of himself and the world in which he lives, and (4) "the methodological problem," i.e., the formal and direct consideration of the presuppositions and the conceptual tools to be used in the study of religion. All of these problem areas are to be interwoven in a structure for which, in particular, Mircea Eliade's *The Sacred and the Profane* and *Primitives to Zen* provide the basic thread of continuity for the following major topics:

1. The variety of religion and religion forms: the problem of tradition and form
2. The nature of religion
3. The meaning and importance of myth for understanding religion: myth in primitive psychology
4. Myth as a religious form
5. Ritual as a religious form
6. Ritual: initiation and celebration
7. Sacred space

8. Sacred time
9. Nature, cosmos and history
10. Religious experience
11. Modes of perception
12. Traditional religious thought, Western scientific thought, and contemporary modes of perception
13. Secularization
14. The old and the new

Florida State University's "Introduction" is similarly designed to emphasize the discipline or method, as well as to indicate the scope of the field. "It is not intended as a substitute for the study of world religions, theology, or the philosophy of religion." Rather, "the focus of the course is on religion, not religions," with the intention of acquainting the student with "the complex problems and issues which arise in the attempt to understand religious phenomena in their human context." The beginning is made with an analysis of the nature of religion, using Eliade's *The Sacred and the Profane* as "the foundation book for the approach to the structure and meaning of religious phenomena." The course then goes on to three major topics in the field. The second focus is the "forms of religion," or the history and literature of religion, using as illustrations selections from the Jewish-Christian scriptures (the book of Deuteronomy) and a devotional classic from the Indian religious tradition (the Bhagavad Gita). The attempt here is to deal with "the problems that arise when one tries to understand 'religion' through religious traditions." The third area of concentration is the religious thinker, specifically Martin Buber (*I and Thou*), identified as the most influential religious thinker of the first half of the twentieth century. In the final section, attention is turned to religion and culture, drawing on the widely acclaimed novel by Malamud, *The Fixer,* as "material for studying the relation between religion and the cultural forms in which religious patterns are manifested."[3]

A related format is found in Princeton University's "Introduction to the Study of Religion," but with a wider range of methodological options developed in readings from Wach, Durkheim, Evans-Pritchard, Frazer, DeVries, Levy-Bruhl, Otto, Weber, Freud, James, Levi-Strauss, Eliade, and Kitagawa. These are deployed in a series of topics also emphasizing the multi-disciplinary approaches:

1. Origin and development of religion: theories of origin
2. Origin and development: primitive mentality and the formation of monotheism
3. Origin and development: cultural stages and social transformation
4. Religious experience: experience and expression
5. Sociology of religion

6. Psychology of religion
7. Myth: cognitive and social significance
8. Myth: myth and ritual
9. Ritual: sacrifice and initiation
10. Symbolism
11. Comparative methods: typology and structuralism
12. Historical methods

In the course patterns just described, materials are drawn naturally from a variety of religious traditions, with strong emphasis on archaic or primitive religions. In a somewhat different kind of introductory course, we find less explicit emphasis on methodological problems as providing structure for the study and a more direct relation to the variety of the developed religions. At one level, these recall the attempt in the older "world religions" courses to exhibit the fundamental characteristics of the great religious traditions, but the treatment is topical or problematic rather than a seriatim review of the religions. Recently developed courses at Yale and North Carolina are valuable illustrations of these tendencies.

Yale's "The Phenomenon of Religion in East and West," a year-long course, combines the study of four major topics—religion and society; scripture, tradition, and change; religious experience and its communication; problems of religious diversity—with a promising experimental pattern of teaching. In each of the four units, after several weeks of lectures and readings, including always a lecture or more on methodology, each student chooses a two-week seminar on a specific topic. The topics go beyond the previous course material and are often only indirectly related to it, thus requiring further research and synthesis on the part of the student. The resultant course outline (with a few illustrations given of the kinds of materials assigned) is of particular interest:

I Religion and Society
1. Islam and the idea of community (including readings on black power and black Muslims)
2. The Buddhist community
3. Christendom (examples from the Byzantine empire and Catholicism and national tradition in South America)
4. American denominations (Herberg)
5. The Jewish People
6. Religious ethics (including discussions of war and moral discourse, and Muslim, Hindu, and Confucian ethics)
7. Religion in primitive cultures
8. Sociological study of religion

A. Seminars: The first amendment and the legal status of a denomination; conscientious objection in America; theology and revolution; Islam and modernity in Turkey.

II Scripture, Tradition and Change

1. "Scripture" in China
2. "Scripture" in India (Bhagavad Gita)
3. The scriptural tradition in Islam
4. Old Testament
5. The Jewish scriptural tradition (Talmud; Rashi)
6. New Testament
7. Reformation (readings from Luther, Calvin, Riedmann)
8. Catholic renewal (Vatican II excerpts)
9. Modernity and scripture (O.T., N.T. in current study: *Inherit the Wind*)

B. Seminars: First century Messianism; ancient Hebrew interpretations of Hebrew tradition; quests for the historical Jesus; comparison of Calvin and Tolstoy.

III Religious Experience and Its Communication

1. The Individual (*Markings* - Dag Hammarskjöld)
2. Mysticism (Islamic mystics; Eckhart; St. Theresa; Zohar)
3. Christians on the Self (Augustine; J. Edwards)
4. Psychological study of religion
5. The Self in Hinduism
   5.1 The Self in Buddhism
6. Classical conceptions of God (Hick, Maimonides, Kant, Anselm)
   6.1 Modern theology and conceptions of God (Tillich, Barth, Hic)
7. Meaning in life and death (*Cry the Beloved Country*)
   7.1 Evil as a problem for faith (*Gates of the Forest*, Frost, J. Royce, Rubemstein)
8. Myth and mystery (Eliade, Rahner, Babylonian myths)
9. Symbolization in ritual
10. The vocabulary of religious art
11. Musical settings of the Mass

C. Seminars: religious autobiography; Christian experiences of conversion; Jung and the I-Ching; criteria for evaluating drug-induced experiences as religious.

IV Problems of Religious Diversity

1. Historical influences and interactions of religions
2. Interfaith opinion from polemic to dialogue (*City of Wrong*)
3. Theories of the nature of religion
4. Religious pluralism and the future (*A Case of Conscience*, Cox, H. G. MacPherson)

D. Seminars: theories of religion in classical antiquity; the Jewish experience in America; Christian-Jewish ecumenism and the state of Israel; religion in Japan since World War II.

The University of North Carolina's Introduction to Religion is focused in a more limited way on the theme, how religious man organizes time and society in different cultural epochs, with the following overall design;

1. Introduction to phenomenology of religion
   1.1 contemporary criticisms of religion (Freud)
2. Myth, cult and culture in tribal societies (*Book of the Hopi*)
3. Horizontal expansion of archaic religions (Eliade)
4. From cyclical time to timelessness: the rise of Oriental religions
   4.1 Hinduism (H. Zimmer)
   4.2 The feeling of Asian religion (H. Hesse)
5. From cyclical time to history: the rise of Occidental religions
   5.1 Hebrew beginnings (*Genesis; Exodus*)
   5.2 Christian beginnings (*Matthew*)
   5.3 Medieval civilization (Aquinas, *Treatise on Laws*)
   5.4 Reformation (Luther, *Christian Liberty*)
6. From religious roots to secular civilization (Weber, *Protestant Ethic*)
7. Agony of the contemporary world (*After Auschwitz*)

In both of the illustrations just cited, definite attempts are made to relate the study of traditional religion to the experience of the contemporary world. That theme, however, is more explicitly characteristic of still other introductory patterns, in which the major focus is found in the confrontation with the existential questions raised in religion and/or in the religious dimensions of contemporary culture.

In Bucknell University's "Contemporary Forms of Faith," for example, the forms include both traditional and non-traditional patterns, examined through modern treatises on the meaning and nature of religion as such and/or the meaning and nature of some specific "religious" view of reality. One version of the course offers the following outline:

I Introduction
   A. Definition of "religion" (Tillich)
   B. Definition of "religious studies"

II Analysis of various forms of contemporary faith
   A. Non-traditional

1. Psychoanalysis (Freud, *Future of an Illustior* and *Civilization and Its Discontents*)
2. Dialectical Materialism (Marx and Engels)
3. Existentialism (Camus, *The Plague, The Myth of Sisyphus, The Rebel*)

B. Traditional: Judaism
   1. Jewish identity after Auschwitz
   2. Nature of the Jewish tradition
   3. A contemporary statement (Borowitz)
   4. Judaism and Christianity

III Relation of religion and science (Barbour)

Dickinson College's "Western religion and contemporary culture" is even more explicitly aimed at the problems of personal faith in the contemporary cultural context. Its stated objective is "to investigate the perennial religious questions as these are posed and answered in our own day, with particular reference to the interaction between the Judaeo-Christian tradition and contemporary culture."

The plan of the course thus takes up the following areas:

1. The Human Condition: three statements of man's plight taken from contemporary literature raise the fundamental problem of human existence and its ultimate meaning. (Salinger, *The Catcher in the Rye;* Kafka, *The Trial;* Camus, *The Plague.*)
2. The response of Faith: an analysis — what faith is and what it is not; its symbols, its types, its truth, the life of faith. (Tillich, *The Dynamics of Faith.*)
3. Faith and Religion: a case study of a believer's struggle to define the relevance of religion in our day. (Bonhoeffer, *Letters and Papers from Prison.*)
4. The Faith-Community and the World: an examination of five possible patterns of encounter between religion and culture. (Niebuhr, *Christ and Culture.*)
5. The Religious Response to Moral Evils in Contemporary Society: racism, war, economic imperialism. (Gavin, *Crisis Now;* Grier & Cobbs, *Black Rage;* Ward, *The Lopsided World.*)

A feature clearly visible in the scheme just noted is the attempt to expand the consciousness of the meaning of the word "religion," to include many quite non-traditional forms of religious expression. That is also explicit in another version of the Bucknell course, in which Norman O. Brown's *Life Against Death* is used as an instance of psychoanalytic reconstruction of faith, "Faith and Eroticism."

The goal of expanding the religious consciousness is also one of the aims stated for an introduction to religion devised at Southern Methodist University: "to broaden and deepen the student's awareness of different ways in which people have been and are religious," "to stimulate the student's sense that religion is not so much a static phenomenon, e.g., a dogma, as a process of becoming —that is, a personal, social, and cosmic power through which man may actualize the highest (ultimate) reality for him," and "to provide a basis through exposure to various religion patterns upon which the student can make a reflective judgment about what religion may mean to him." Thus the course attempts to avoid imposing the basic concepts of any one religious tradition on religious phenomena as a whole, and also to draw data from as wide a range as possible both historically and geographically, thus including materials drawn both from traditionally recognized religious writings and from contemporary "secular" Western writings that have a religious function. The result is a sequence of study organized around seven possible "ultimate concerns" or ways of being religious—four of them are conventionally religious, three are secular options (i.e., lacking in specifically ultimate claims yet providing or promising a framework for life). In the following partial description each segment includes not only examples and interpretative or phenomenological analysis but also a statement of the "problematics" drawing on contemporary writers:

1. Personal experience of the holy (devotion, prayer, ecstatic experiences)
   Illustrations from the Bible, W. James *et al.*, Problematics: Otto, Flew, *et al.*

2. Myth-Sacrament (sacred action and holy living)
   Phenomenological analysis of sacred action in ritual as related to the holy story and to the life-world of the believer. Problematics: Freud, Jung, Islam, Van Harvey

3. Daily living expressing the cosmic law (perfect man as an expression of God's will)
   Hinduism (Radhakrishnan), Confucianism; Islam Problematics: P. Berger, *et al.*

4. Spiritual freedom through discipline (mysticism, yoga)
   Phenomenology of mysticism
   Buddhist, Islamic, Christian mysticism
   Problematics: Murphy, Fingarette, Jung, Feigel

5. Social-Economic justice as ultimate concern
   Rousseau and Dewey
   Revolutionaries (Thomas Paine, A. Koestler)
   Civil rights
   Problematics of ethics and religion

6. The senses as the way to personal fulfillment
   Advocates of sensuous rediscovery and of consciousness expanding drugs. Problematics of salvation
   through "letting go"
7. New life through Technocracy
   Genetics, social control
   Problematics: Bertalanffy, Cox, Brunner, Heschel.

An impressive example of concentration on non-traditional
and para-religious elements is offered in Indiana University's Introduction to Religion and Culture. After preliminary discussion of the
nature of religious experience and the role of religion in the formation of culture, the body of the course consists chiefly of an examination of unofficial, non-traditional and indeed anti-traditional expressions of religion in contemporary culture, accompanied sec-
ondarily (chiefly through lectures but partly through readings in
such figures as de Rougemont, McGill and Buber) by commentary
in which theological framework and perspective are provided:

I Religion in Culture
1. Nature of religious experience (Van der Leeuw; examples
   from Genesis, Exodus; Malraux)
2. Religion and the Formation of a Culture (Cox, Berger,
   Niebuhr, Bergson, O'Dea)
3. Religion and the Secularization of a Culture (Cox, Berger,
   O'Dea)

II Evidence of Religion in Contemporary American Culture
1. The influence of official religion (Herberg, Lenski)
2. The influence of "unofficial" religious patterns
   a. The religious element in sexual encounter (de Rouge-
      mont)
   b. The religious element in personal encounter (Buber)
   c. The religious element in man's encounter with death
      (Tolstoy; Gorer)
   d. The religious fascination with destructive power
      (McGill)
   e. The religious element in politics (Bellah)
      1. Radical right (Hofstadter: *The Paranoid Style in
         American Politics*)
      2. Conservative (Babylonian Creation Myth, and the
         Los Angeles Times on Chicago riots after the death
         of Martin Luther King)
      3. New Left (Fanon, Malcolm X; student anti-establish-
         mentarianism on the Left — Roszak)
   f. The Western fascination with Eastern religion (Herri-
      gel: *Zen Including Zen in the Art of Archery*)

Finally, Waterloo Lutheran University's "Contemporary Religious Issues" may be cited as an illustration not only of an unusually broad spectrum of contemporary religious and cultural issues, focusing on the problem of the understanding of man, his nature, his situation, and his destiny, but also incorporating a wide variety of techniques, including debates, films, field trips, and an appearance of the case of the musical "Hair" to inquire into the religious dimensions of that drama. The 1970-1971 version included:

Introduction:	Film ("Patterns of the Mind")
Man, his nature, situation and destiny:	Man from a musician's viewpoint (outside lecture)
	Man from a humanist's viewpoint (outside lecture)
	Man from a psychologist's viewpoint (outside lecture)
	Film ("The Pawnbroker")
	Dialog (Man from Eastern and Western viewpoints) Two lecturers
	Summary
Is God necessary for modern man:	Film ("Through a Glass Darkly")
	Seminars
	Debate (involving two philosophy department members)
Social Issues:	Birth control (outside lecturer)
	Sexual relationships — seminars — film ("Monica")
	Sex and religion
	Eschatological nudity (outside lecturer)
The Individual in and/or versus society:	Two lectures, one by a sociologist and one by a political scientist
Social change and conflict:	Film ("Through Conflict to Negotiation: The Alinsky Approach")
Protest:	Debate (an M-P and a historian)
Poverty and affluence:	Film ("The Best Damn Fiddler")
Technology:	Film ("Murrow-Oppenheimer Interview")
	Field trip to a tobacco factory
Mass Media:	Panel
Response:	Possible life styles: panel of students

2. Styles of Religion Curricula: Six Illustrations

The changing patterns of undergraduate religion curricula do not always result from design. The definition of areas considered to be important may often be determined by such "accidental" determinants as the competencies of the faculty who are already present or by the inability to make appointments in precisely the areas intended, as well as by the changing interests of faculty and students. Nevertheless, there are obvious major differences that do result from the orientations of the institution and the intentions of the departmental planners. A regular feature of the new styles is the abandonment of the "seminary triad"—biblical, historical, systematic—as the pattern for organizing studies. That triad has represented a long and distinguished tradition of scholarship. But it emerged explicitly in the context of the religious community's interest in professional preparation, which is not a function of the new styles of religion programs. Some sense of the range of possibilities can be gained simply by setting alongside each other half a dozen patterns of departmental course offerings drawn from widely varying types of institutions.

a. Hardin Simmons is a Baptist institution offering a major in Bible within the Department of Bible and Philosophy. It represents the quite traditional pattern of emphasis on biblical studies in conservative Protestant-related institutions.[4] All students at the college are required to take two courses in Bible and prerequisites for admission to the undergraduate major are Old Testament and New Testament surveys, together with Baptist Doctrine and Practice and the Work of the Minister. Majors must also take a historical survey of religious education or a course in organizations for religious education. The orientation toward practical ministerial service is evident.

Apart from Greek language courses, which do not count toward the degree in religion, the program of the department is divided into Bible, Philosophy, and Religion, on the following pattern:

Bible: 8 courses, including: Baptist Doctrine and Practice, Comparative Theology (teaching of the major denominations of America), 2 Bible seminars.

Philosophy: 6 courses, including: Introduction to Philosophy; Ethics; Logic; History of Philosophy; Contemporary Philosophy; Philosophy of the Christian Religion.

Religion: Courses including: Work of the Minister; Evangelism; Sermon Preparation; Christian History; Christianity in America; Christian Missions; World Religions . . . with special emphasis on the superiority of Christianity as the final religion of mankind; Christianity and Modern Problems; Church and Denominational Activities.

b. Saint Xavier College (Chicago) offers a characteristic program in theological and religious studies. An institution that has a predominantly Catholic student body, it is interested in more deeply exposing the student to his own religious heritage, thus par-

101

ticular attention is paid to Roman Catholic studies, though the six-hour theology requirement of the College is based on the conviction that the study of the religious experience in the heritage of man ought to be an integral aspect of any liberal education. The requirement may be filled by a two-course sequence in Christian and non-Christian ideologies of the West since 1500, or a sequence in contemporary world religions. The goal of the theology program is to "provide the student with a basic knowledge of biblical studies, and the history of theology and contemporary religious and theological topics and problems." The resultant spectrum of course offerings emphasizes theology and the history of Christianity:

100 level:
Directions in Modern Catholic Thought I and II (101-102)
Christian and Secular Thought in Modern Times (103)
Contemporary Religious Issues (104)
Religions of Man I and II (105-106)

200 level:
Old Testament Life and Literature
New Testament Life and Literature
Major Trends in Christian Thought to 1500
God and Secularity
Christian Ethics
Judaism Past and Present
Orthodox Christianity

300 level:
Life and Teachings of Jesus
The Bible as Literature
Contemporary Movements in Roman Catholicism
Revelation and the Development of Dogma
The Liturgical Dimension of Man in Society
Basic Ecclesiological Themes and Problems
Seminar on Moral Problems
Twentieth Century Roman Catholic Theology
Roman Catholic and Protestant Modernism
Religion and Culture in America
Psychology and Religion
Sociology of Religion
Greek Religion and Mythology
Contemporary Religious Education
Independent Study
Theology Seminar

c. The University of Detroit Department of Religious Studies, as even the name of the department suggests, represents a quite different determination of the areas of study — as well as an extraordinarily large number of courses offered, 46 in all. The fields represent a combination of traditional emphasis on the history of Christianity and on Christian thought with a high degree of innovation in the definition of new areas.

The 8 *introductory courses* (i.e., those which can be taken as a first course) include:

Sacred Texts in a Secular World
Social and Political Protest in Ancient Israel
Problem of Jesus: History and Myth
Christian Existence: "offers an updated view of the Catholic faith"
Myths of Faith and Doubt in the Modern Novel: Hesse, Golding, and Dostoyevsky
Religion and Urban Conflicts: case study of churches in Detroit
Introduction to Asian Religious Thought

The 24 *intermediate courses* include in part:

Media and Message in the New Testament
St. John
Basic Religious Problems
Modern Views of Christ: A Critique
The Church: Movement or Structure: Vatican II and the new ecclesiology
Early Medieval Christian Society: Growth of Christianity 500-1000: conflict of Mediterranean and "Germanic" cultures
Understanding Protestantism
A Theology of Woman
Teilhard de Chardin
Jewish Medieval Thought
Jews and Judaism in Western History
Theology and Literature: Utopias, Anti-Utopias, and a theology of the future
The Modern Political Novel: *Catch 22: Confessions of Nat Turner: The Possessed*
The Ethics of Revolution and Protest (also philosophy course)
Comparative Religion I
Comparative Religion II
Hinduism, Past and Present
Religions of Non-Literate Societies

Among the 14 *mixed undergraduate/graduate courses* are to be counted:

Message and Meaning of Apocalyptic
Marxism and Christianity

The Gregorian Reform (of the 11th and 12th centuries)
Nazism and the Response of the Christian Churches
Jewish Literature
Cults in Collision: Pagan and Christian Britain from the end
of Roman period to the Age of the Vikings
History of Religions: Methods and approaches in the comparative study of religion

d. The newly developing Department of Religious Studies in a state university, the University of Montana, presents a radically different approach. Here religion is understood at every point in the closest possible connection with study that is important through all the humane and social disciplines. Three foci are proposed: "The Modern Sensibility," i.e., the question of how modern man, especially the modern American, senses the world; "Language and Tradition," i.e., the way tradition enters into the constitution of a present reality frame and the way the constitution of reality "frames in" other times and places; and "The Religious Conceptuality," i.e., the way man's sensibility attains self-understanding in the construction of conceptual frames. In these three foci the aim is to focus on what might be taken as the religious aspect, but with the recognition that no neat distinction can be drawn between the religious and the secular aspects of culture.

Consonant with these principles, the design for future faculty development, which envisages the eventual introduction of graduate studies in religion at the University, embodies the following pattern. Beginning with two senior faculty in the areas of philosophical theology (including the history of Western religious thought) and of Hellenistic languages and literature (with concentration on New Testament studies), additional appointments would come in the following order, with the interdepartmental connections indicated: a scholar in one oriental language and religious tradition, overlapping the present staff and perhaps jointly appointed with the history department; a specialist in ethics and/or aesthetics; a colleague trained in American history and letters, again in connection with the history department; a joint appointment with English in religion and literature; a second person in biblical studies with special competence in ancient Near East and Old Testament; a colleague with a second oriental language and a second oriental tradition; a specialist in linguistics; a colleague in nineteenth century European religious history and tradition, to complement the American specialization; a specialist in Graeco-Roman religions, with training in classics; a Judaic scholar; and finally a specialist in religion and the arts, working in conjunction with the school of fine arts.

Course areas offered to date reflect a partial realization of those goals:

Introduction to the Study of Religion

Jewish and Christian Literature of Late Antiquity
Religion in America
History of the Ancient Near East
Parables: Jesus and Kafka
The Legacy of Paul
The Rise of Historical Consciousness in the Ancient Near East
Christianity and Marxism
Religious Ethics
Contemporary Theology
The Bible in the American Tradition
Contemporary Biblical Interpretation
Religion in the Hellenistic Period
Rhetoric in Classical Greek and Semitic Literature
Religion and Social Reality
Human Spirit and Technology
God-language in Nineteenth Century Thought
Philosophy of Religion
Religion in Contemporary Culture
Religion and Political Imagination
Atheism in the Modern World
Systematic Symbolics
Studies in Language and Tradition
Problems in Religious Studies

e. Western Michigan, with one of the long-established state university departments of religion, has also developed a distinctive and self-conscious style. As we noted in reference to the introductory course, the object of study is the phenomena of religion conceived as a definable generic aspect of human experience. In the context of the consideration of the nature and history of man's encounter with the sacred, the data of religion are approached in four different ways and courses are ordered under four specific fields of study.

In the field of "historical studies" the focus is on the development of religion in different periods and places. The field of "morphological and phenomenological studies" approaches religious phenomena "through the study of recurring religious patterns, forms, or structures as they can be discerned regardless of time or place. This field is concerned with the structure of religion rather than with the history of religion." The field of "methodological studies" is "analytical and critical in its approach to religion." An important element in this field is a disciplined consideration of how to study religion. The field of "constructive studies" is especially concerned with "the power of religion as it explores issues and proposals in the contemporary religious situation, the significance of new religious forms, and the religious possibilities for the future which emerge in and through ecumenical and cross-cultural perspectives."

(An undergraduate major in religion must include the introductory course described in Section 1 above, two courses from "Historical Studies" and one each from the other three areas. At least two upper level seminars must be included.)

The resulting spectrum of course areas is one in which careful balance is given to the various pre-historic and historic traditions and to the varieties of approaches:

1. Historical Studies

   Prehistoric and Primitive Religions
   Protohistoric Religions: Ancient Near East, Greece, Rome, and Meso America
   Religion in the Indian Tradition
   Religion in the Chinese and Japanese Traditions
   African Religions
   The Christian Tradition
   The Jewish Tradition
   The Islamic Tradition
   Historical Studies in Religion (seminar)

2. Morphological and Phenomological Studies in Religion

   The Morphology and Phenomenology of Religion
   Myth and Ritual
   Religious Forms in Modern Literature
   Morphological and Phenomenological Studies in Religion (seminar)

3. Methodological Studies in Religion

   The Philosophy of Religion
   The History of the Study of Religion
   Methodological Studies in Religion (seminar)

4. Constructive Studies in Religion

   Studies in Contemporary Theology
   The Religious Quest in Modern Literature
   Religion and Social Ethics
   Constructive Studies in Religion (seminar)

f. Finally, a recent restructuring in a private non-sectarian institution, Pomona College, reflects still another way of seeking to meet the legitimate interests of the students, both serious academic interests and ill-defined quests for spirituality, as well as to abandon traditional groupings around historical periods and development of religious tradition. Emphasis is put on comparative analysis of Eastern and Western perspectives, on literary criticism, intellectual history, phenomenological investigations and classics, and on the identification of loci in contemporary culture around which serious problems gather in the study of religion. A further basic principle has been the judgment that the program should not be tailored to the expectation of large numbers of majors, thus it should not take the form of a highly structured curriculum in which budding specialists move steadily from beginnings to more complex levels.

The consequence has been a radical reconstruction of course offerings, on the following lines:[5]

Introduction: Sacred Texts, Spiritual Experiences, Critical Thinkers

Courses on the primary and secondary literature in the field:
The Study of Religion
The Biblical Heritage
The Oriental Heritage

Courses on topics in religious life and thought:
The Life and Death of God: Mystery, Myth and Theory
The World, The City of God, and the Problem of Justice
Ecstatic Vision and Prophetic Word
Transformation and Utopia
Redemption and Freedom: Faith or Satori?

Courses in specialized research and guided reading:
Selected Topics
Senior Seminar
Senior Thesis

3. The Undergraduate Major—Another Essay in Diversity

The undergraduate major has been discussed earlier in this volume by Professor Slater, as well as briefly in our more statistical review. Some further account is needed, however, of the diversity and fluidity—one may speak of both innovation and disorder—in the changing views of the major.

New definitions of the appropriate *content* of the major are naturally closely interwoven with the concepts of the proper introduction to religious studies and the new style of programs just reviewed. The special problems of major requirements turn largely on the question "for what?" "What will you do with a major in religion?" "To what extent, if at all, is such a major viewed as vocational preparation?"

In an earlier day the religion major, offered mostly in church-related institutions, largely served one of two purposes: undergraduate level professional preparation for careers in religious education or other kinds of church work, or pre-professional study leading to subsequent seminary education. The latter aim, of course, was primarily characteristic of Protestant institutions, since training for the Roman Catholic priesthood was carried on in separate college level seminaries rather than in the liberal arts colleges. The suitability of the undergraduate major in religion for pre-seminary training was for a time seriously questioned by the leaders in theological education, partly because of the earlier poor quality of much undergraduate instruction in religion, partly because of the judgment that the best pre-seminary training was a broad liberal arts education, including philosophy, history, literature, social science and language, with the specialized studies in Bible and theology to come at the graduate level only.[6]

These former vocational purposes have declined relatively in importance, though they have not vanished and continue to persist strongly in conservative institutions (see the illustration of the Hardin-Simmons program, Section 2 above). Indeed, with the improvement in quality of undergraduate religious studies and in the broadening of their scope, it is widely argued that religion is at least as valid as any other area for "a broad liberal arts education," and furthermore that it is altogether artificial for the prospective minister to postpone fundamental studies in religion and theology until after college. It is also true that in recent decades many students have first come to consider the possibility of careers in religious service, not as a result of prior religious training, but primarily because of the study undertaken at the college level. Further, students often enter theological schools for reasons precisely comparable to those that have led to the study of religion at the undergraduate level, quite without a precise vocational commitment of orientation. It remains true, however, (a) that the importance of undergraduate major as pre-professional training is declining relatively, and (b) that the character of that pre-professional study of religion is tending to become less and less a concentration on Bible and the history of Christian thought and more an inclusive and diversified study of religious phenomena of many sorts.

A more recent vocational orientation for the religion major is graduate study leading to careers in teaching and research in religion. Earlier (Part II) this aim was shown to be considered of moderate importance by department chairmen in all types of institutions. The emergence of this goal was particularly a phenomenon of the 1960's as colleges and universities expanded, and in private non-sectarian and public institutions the study of religion expanded even more rapidly. With the slowing down of the rate of college expansion in the 1970's and the surplus of teachers that has appeared with dramatic suddenness, this function of the undergraduate religion concentration will also surely decline relatively in importance. Yet it has come to occupy a permanent place in the spectrum and cannot be ignored. Especially in this area do we encounter the problems of discipline and cohesion to which Professor Slater has called attention. The changing of patterns of entrance into graduate study in religion, particularly the growing tendency to bypass the professional degree and proceed directly from college to graduate studies, together with the expansion of the conception of the field have greatly intensified the problems of coherence in religion. One example of the difficulty has been the abandonment so far of all attempts to devise a Graduate Record Examination in the field of religion, even though preliminary explorations have been initiated several times in recent decades. Attempts were dropped partly because of uncertainty concerning the numbers of students who might be expected to take such an exam, but equally because of the difficulty of defining the proper foci and allowing for all the varieties of undergraduate programs.

Granted that the field of religion does not allow a vertical structure comparable to chemistry, physics or biology, some kinds of ordering must nonetheless be devised. Moreover, there are emergent tendencies that may be leading toward a consensus as to the appropriate constituents of a coherent and disciplined undergraduate program of study, when that is conceived as the basis upon which students may build advanced studies in religion. Three sorts of ingredients appear to be of special prominence. First, a responsible pattern of study of religious phenomena cannot be limited simply to one religious tradition, but must include serious attention to two or more, preferably from diverse cultural traditions. Second, there must be serious and extensive attention to the question of general theory and method in the interpretation of religion, including historical, philosophical, literary, phenomenological, psychological and sociological perspectives and styles of approach. No student, of course, can be expected to immerse himself in all of these styles, but a diversity is essential—and the range of possibilities for such specialization is now broadened to include the Eastern religions, primitive religions, religion and the social sciences, religion and the arts, and the like. Finally, such programs would also seem necessarily to include the beginning of serious study in the relevant languages.

More recently still, another vocational option for the undergraduate major has appeared on the horizon and it may be expected to grow in importance: namely, the teaching of religion at the secondary school level. What sort of organized program of religious studies will be relevant here? The novelty and experimental nature of secondary school study in religion make all projections and norms extremely hazardous. But it seems safe to say that the kind of concentration and focus necessary as background for graduate studies cannot directly be the model. Doubtless the study of the several religious traditions in their inner coherence and historical development will be important components. Equally important are likely to be the combinations of religion with other fields of study. If the patterns of public school religious studies emerging in

109

Florida, Pennsylvania, and Nebraska are harbingers of the future, it seems that combinations of religion and literature and of religion and the social sciences are destined to wax in significance — since in the Florida scheme the study of religion is incorporated into existing social studies courses, and the Pennsylvania courses in religious literature of the West and East must be offered in the literature branch of the schools and taught by persons qualified as literature teachers. Thus the appropriate patterns may be joint majors with one or other of these areas or perhaps the incorporation of religious studies as a minor area.

Though we cannot predict what will happen in secondary school programs in religion, it is likely that all three of the vocationally oriented conceptions of the undergraduate major will in the long run play only a relatively modest role. Of greater importance, at least numerically and perhaps conceptually, will be the attempt to interpret a concentration in religious studies as one mode among others of general liberal arts education in the humanities and the social sciences, conceivably even as a dominant mode for the exploration of human culture. Here the values assigned to vocational preparation tend to approach zero. Here too the protest against the fashioning of an undergraduate program after the traditional seminary triad is intensified. The goal is not in fact to fashion experts in religion, but to use the "religious" as a way of pressing into the broadest questions of man's values and culture.

Here the problem of a "discipline" becomes acute. Students seem to enter religion majors for the most diverse reasons (often quite unrelated to the purposes that faculty envisage), and many go on to professional training in law, medicine, and social work, or to graduate study in other fields. In not a few undergraduate institutions, it should be noted, religious programs are the only loci for extensive work in Asian studies.

One option, of course, as in the Pass Major at the University of Toronto, is the pure cafeteria, with no requirement other than a certain number of courses among those listed as religious studies. This may be a path increasingly attractive to undergraduates, especially those whose real preference would be not to be required to have any structure at all in their undergraduate studies. Few departments, however, are willing to go quite so far, wanting usually to hold both to some pattern of distribution among the various areas of religious study and to a definable concentration within the field, so as to provide at least a minimal structure and depth. A good illustration of the former requirement is the University of Pennsylvania major which presupposes a general introduction to religion and substantive work in more than one religious tradition, requiring an examination at the end of the junior year on (1) the history and morphology of two major religious traditions of the world, and (2) theories and methods in the interpretation of religion. (The honors major calls in addition for a concentration of at least four courses in a given area, e.g., the religions of India or European religious thought through the medieval period, and a senior thesis.)

In several of the innovative curricular styles described earlier (e.g., Pomona, Montana, Western Michigan), nontraditional foci for the undergraduate major are prominent. A further illustration of a modest step in that direction, though also preserving traditional patterns, is the undergraduate program structure of the University of Santa Clara. Two course sequences are provided: one predominantly Roman Catholic, the other "neutral." Every student at Santa Clara chooses a set of distributionally required religion courses from one of these sequences.

Prospective majors are required to form a "core sequence" from the following courses: Introduction to the Old Testament; Introduction to the New Testament; Christian Origins; Religious Symbol and Myth; Christian Anthropology; Theology of Christian Community; World Religions; Christian Ethics; and Christian Liturgy. Having completed the core sequence, a student may choose to concentrate his major in one of three general areas: Scripture, Theology, and Religion and Society. Though no student is obliged to focus his major in these areas, he may if he chooses work out in consultation with an advisor a coherent set of courses in any one of them, or in some other area, e.g., Religion and the Arts.

Santa Clara also requires a number of extra-departmental courses for all majors. These include three lower-division courses in philosophy, two of which must deal with the history of philosophy, two courses in fine arts, and two courses in history. In addition, beginning majors must demonstrate "competence in written expression" by submitting an essay, which may fulfill a course requirement; and all majors, by the middle of the senior year must pass a foreign language test, administered by the Department of Religious Studies.

Finally, we may recall the long standing pattern developed at Princeton University, providing for formal joint majors between religion and history, religion and philosophy, and religion and literature. The combination religion and philosophy has, of course, had a long history in the college study of religion generally. What is relatively novel in recent decades has been the expansion of such formal bridges to include not only the social sciences and literature and the arts, but also such areas as urban studies and religion and science. These are supported also by tendencies toward a definition of religious studies as inherently interdisciplinary, or at least cross-disciplinary (see below, Section 4).

In sum, innovation in respect of the religion major appears to be represented by two closely related trends. First, there is a growing variety in areas of concentration proposed within the field and recognized as equally valid with traditional emphasis on Bible or the history of Christian thought. In addition to areas just cited, these include especially the non-Western religions and a wide range of parareligious phenomena. Second, there is apparently an increasing openness to a strictly "individualized" major, i.e., one in which an undergraduate is free to carve out any constellation of studies, provided he can persuade an advisor that it has some kind of cohesion or coherence.

4. Cross-Disciplinary and Interdisciplinary Study

At many points in the preceding sections we have touched upon efforts to develop the study of religion in the closest interconnections with other "disciplines." It is evident that in the nature of their programs and of individual courses, many departments are in fact cross-disciplinary in character—this even though, as we noted in Part II, very few religion programs are interdepartmental in structure (except for the relatively common joint departments of religion and philosophy and the occasional joint departments of religion and history, or the like). The "interdisciplinary credentials" of religion may indeed be most thoroughly established in the ordinary departmental structures.

Yet it will be useful to look briefly at two efforts to be even more formally interdisciplinary—one in a relatively new religion department that has been experimenting extensively with team taught cross-disciplinary courses, the other in a program maintaining on principle an interdepartmental structure.

At Wright State University (Dayton, Ohio) the Religion Department has from its inception been encouraged to experiment in team-taught cross-disciplinary courses.[7] By 1971 eight such team-taught upper-class courses had been introduced into the curriculum: "The Religious Quest in Contemporary Literature," taught jointly with the English Department; "Evolution," taught with the Biology Department; "Ethics in an Industrial Society," taught with the Business Department; "The Marxist-Christian Dialogue," taught with the Political Science Department; "The Religious Quest in Modern Cinema," taught with the Cinema Department; "The Religious Quest in Contemporary Music," taught with the Music Department; "Religion and Geography in India," taught with the Geography Department; and "Teaching about Religion in the Public Schools," taught with the College of Education. These particular courses grew out of the personal contacts and individual interests of faculty members involved, though with the general encouragement of the administration to develop such courses as seemed desirable and feasible.

The stated principles for the ventures were that such courses "must introduce students to the methodologies of the disciplines involved, along with a comparison, contrast, and critical evaluation of these methodologies." Ways in which the methodologies complement and contradict each other were to be explored and the possibilities of synthesis were to be discussed. The instructors were to approach the courses as fellow explorers with the students rather than cross-disciplinary experts, and were obliged to participate jointly in every aspect of the course, from preparation through final evaluation. Conclusions emerging from these experiments include the following: the team teaching of cross-disciplinary courses increases each participating faculty member's work load. It is much easier to isolate, compare, contrast and criticize different and sometimes conflicting methodologies than it is to synthesize them. Students and faculty discover that many of the methodological problems and conflicts are due to conflicting epistemologies and value systems and that these are the most important areas for cross-disciplinary courses to pursue in depth and at length. In spite of the tendency of students in these experiments to come to the course either as dogmatically loyal to a traditional approach to religion or as rebelling against it, participation in such study does help in breaking down those kinds of dogmatism. It is recognized that the epistemological and value problems must be pursued. Physical science students begin to discover that many of the presuppositions they believed to support "empirically verified epistemologies and value systems" could not in fact be empirically verified. Political science students began to discern for the first time the interrelation of religious, philosophical, political and economic concepts and values. On the other hand, students in the humanities often developed a deeper appreciation for the rigors of the physical and social science methods and were moved to more disciplined searching in their own intellectual pursuits.

Finally, in spite of the fact that all students in these courses had presumably participated in a general education program for freshmen and sophomores, theoretically designed to make students knowledgeable and conversant in the major disciplines of the arts and sciences, there was still much impatience and frustration because of the necessity to introduce each group of specialists to the other's discipline and jargon. It was still necessary, in order not to confound the humanities and social science majors, to deal with scientific information, language, and problems at a level too elementary to suit science majors. On the other hand, philosophical, ethical, theological, socio-economic and political issues had frequently to be presented at a level that seemed primitive to the humanities and social science majors. Students and faculty who have participated in these courses are nonetheless enthusiastic about the approach and believe it is a minor movement within their university towards reuniting academic disciplines which have been erroneously separated and compartmentalized. Also, they have begun to question whether departments are the most wise and effective foundation stones for the university's basic academic structure. In the words of one faculty member, "We are discovering that our departmental fiefdoms are a hindrance to creative scholarship and teaching."

The University of Vermont religion program offers an illustration of a program that has deliberately remained cross-departmental in structure.[8] Religion was recognized as a "proper academic subject matter" with the establishment of the Department of Philosophy and Religion in 1946, with a major in religion being first offered in 1963. The program developed with a comparative and non-theological orientation, with the history of religions as the foundation of the curriculum and Eastern religions receiving more attention than the Western, and religious phenomenology more than religious philosophy or theology. At the time, then, when the general tendency was toward the establishment of religion as an autonomous subject matter, the decision was here made not to separate religion from philosophy, as in many other institutions, but to continue developing the programs within the present joint department. The major arguments for this pattern can be summarized briefly. The principle is to locate religious studies within the "liberal arts community," rather than the graduate school or seminary professionalism, thus to avoid the tendency for the undergraduate college to become "a sub-extension of graduate school professionalism with all its *sui generis* methodologies."

The result is seen as validation of the observation that "some of the most exciting intellectual activity is occurring in the interstices between the disciplines." The maintenance of a joint department structure thus symbolizes the idea of religious studies as a "microcosmic world within the larger amorphous community."

Though the actual course areas themselves are less distinctively cross-disciplinary than many we have encountered in other structures, the overall configuration of study reflects the philosophy of the program. At the beginning questions in the study of religion are introduced through Asian and Western materials respectively, with an attempt to give contexts within which the study of religion can be related to the whole study of man. The next three "foundational" courses explored the societal, experiental, and mythic-symbolic aspects of religion. Courses on specific traditions presuppose this basis. These studies in turn provide resources for intensive consideration of methodology, for specialized studies in religious phenomenologies and figures, for formalized interdisciplinary studies, and for a senior project.

I.Introductory courses
   Introduction to the Study of Religion (two semesters, with with emphasis on Asian or Western religion)

II.Foundational, structural courses
   Religion and Society
   Mysticism, Shamanism, and Possession
   Myth, Symbol, and Ritual
   Philosophy of Religion

III.Courses on specific religious traditions
- A. Western traditions
    - Hebrew Scriptures
    - Post-Bible Judaism
    - Primitive Christianity
    - Hellenistic Religion
    - Modes of Christian Expression
    - Religion in America
- B. Asian Traditions
    - Studies in the Hindu Tradition
    - Studies in the Buddhist Tradition
    - Japanese Religion
    - Chinese Religion and Thought
- C. Folk, Primitive, Secular
    - "Primitive" Religions
    - Sudies in Folk Religion
    - Religion and Secular Culture

IV.Special Topics
- Special Topics
- Readings and Research
- Problems in the History and Phenomenology of Religion

V.Integrative Courses
- Senior Project
- College Honors
- Theory and Method
- Interdisciplinary Seminar

5. New/Old Areas and Methods: Self Instruction; Multi-media; "Participative" Education

a. Experiments at Bucknell University and Florida State University offer samples of largely self-taught and potentially accelerated courses of study. At Bucknell, this pattern was devised as one of three possible options for the introduction to religion—the other two were a "regular" course and an honors section, both taught by the "discussion" or Socratic method, the honors section being more intensive and limited in enrollment. In the "continuous progress" version, an attempt was made to combine freedom for individual study with the structure of a regular course, i.e., to provide self-instruction at the student's own pace in mastery of a given body of material. A series of ten units was specified, at the end of each of which the student sat for an examination, presenting himself at whatever time he wished, provided only that one-half of the course had to be completed by the end of the first semester. That is, a student could accelerate at his pleasure but not proceed more slowly than the specified rate. A relatively elaborate set of rules also detailed minimum standards of performance and the like. This experiment was not judged to be successful and has been given up in the religion course, but proved more attractive and useful in introductory logic and in introduction to psychology.

The Florida State scheme (for the introduction to the study of religion, noted earlier), also provides several routes. Assisted by a set of audio-tutorial tapes, plus a single weekly class meeting for discussion, (1) students may simply complete all assigned readings and take written examinations according to schedule proposed; or (2) they may complete the readings and take the examinations at their own pace, provided that they move faster than the stated schedule. For the latter group, examinations are given individually or in small groups as the students present themselves. Or (3) as a variant of the second option, a student may finish all the reading as quickly as he can and give satisfactory evidence of his progress by examination, then undertake an individual research project in consultation with the instructor. In this case the grade for the course is based mainly on the project, and it is expected that most students electing this route will receive grades higher than those electing the other options.

b. Another pattern of instructional innovation, combining the use of multiple media and team teaching in an introductory study of religion has been developed by the faculty at McMurry College (Abilene, Texas).[9] This experiment was developed on the principle that "individuation" is the educational goal to be sought for each student, and that individuation involves at least four dimensions: awareness, stimulation, data information, and reflection/integration. The content of the course centers in questions of religious meaning, this being developed through: reviews of non-Christian religious responses; general considerations about man, nature, cosmos and religion; traditional and contemporary Christian responses; and a series of contemporary social and individual problems.

Five principal types of activity are incorporated: a constant use of team teaching involving six faculty members and the active participation of students in planning; large class sessions based on team teaching and the employment of a variety of media, including motion pictures and other photographic aids, tapes of music and spoken material, and original slide shows by faculty or students; written assignments for individual students; small permanent preceptorial groups meeting weekly; and a journal kept by each student in which he is asked to record his responses to the material — the journal also being a primary source of critical and evaluative response for faculty members.

The results seem to have been significant arousal of student interest and the development of the ability to respond in depth to the subject matter. More students appear to have been "reached" effectively than by other methods of dealing with large introductory courses.

c. The issue of study about religion versus participation in religion has been raised to another level of debate particularly in the growing explorations of mysticism—obviously a dimension of central importance in religion, Eastern and Western, from the beginning, but one now elevated to new interest both by the undergraduate fascination with Eastern religions and by the influence of the psychedelic sub-culture in contemporary American student life.

In a course designed at Rollins College (by A. Arnold Wettstein), for example, the ideal of "participative education" is explicitly adopted, on the principle that "to avoid the pressing personal questions about which students agonize or in which they are existentially interested, is to make the academic process not only uninteresting but irrelevant, worthy of the contempt it frequently incurs." Here a distinction is made between primary and secondary goals. The former include: What is mysticism? Who is a mystic? What is the character of his special experience? What are the common and/or distinctive mystical elements in the various religious traditions? How is mysticism related to contemporary world views and modern cultural forms (e.g., drugs)? How does one interpret the mystic's claims and values? The answering of such questions remains basic. "Second order" aims, then, include not only developing a methodology appropriate to the subject, broadening knowledge about the particular religions studied, and preparation for further study, but also "increased sensitivity on the part of participating students," widening appreciation by "virtue of new frames of reference as well as methods;" and "provision of a setting in which self-awareness through meditative practices and group discussions related to mystical experience."

In relation notably to these latter aims an attempt is being made to resolve the "dilemma" between an "objective" and a "committed approach" to religious issues, through study "*in* not *about* mysticism, guided by a participative educational method." This involves emphasis on "the practice of meditative techniques by which the student seeks the mystic's perspective, or at least some empathy with his views;" exposure to the variety of mystical traditions and interpretations; and dialogue with others of differing experiences and commitments as a means to finding one's own way; as well as responsibility in the planning of the study itself.

This particular course was designed for a five-week Intersessional term, during which the study is the sole academic occupation of a limited number (25) of students. A course in world religions is presupposed. Students are asked to develop a plan of meditation (background reading from Bradford Smith's Meditation). Daily journals are kept, turned in weekly and reviewed by the instructor. The class is organized into smaller groups for intensive discussion and group meditation. There is optional participation in encounter training sessions. The core of the course, however, is the daily class sessions, which take various forms. The initial object of attention is reading in the literature of mysticism both traditional and contemporary descriptions and interpretations (including drug-induced experiences). Common characteristics of mystical experience are sought and interpretative reference frames (e.g., neo-Platonism, Vedanta) are considered. The literature of psychedelic experience is reviewed. The relation of mystic experience to cultural expression (especially in art) and to ethics is considered. Following a two-and-a-half day retreat for study, discussion, and encounter sessions in a relatively unstructured experience, the final week is devoted to summation and review, turning on the question of the meaning of the mystical.

d. A markedly different, but not altogether discontinuous, study of mysticism appears in the Wesleyan University course "Mystical Consciousness and Mystical Utopias," developed by Jeremy Zwelling. This is designed as a phenomenological and historical evaluation of the consciousness of individual mystics and the communities which they establish. It takes up mystical systems and utopian communities of late antiquity (Philo, Therapeutae, Gnostics), of the Medieval period (Joachim, left wing Franciscans, Brethren of the Free Spirit) and of more recent times (Indian Peyote cults, Hasidism, Huxley, LSD communes). Obviously a novel and distinctive element here is the exploration of the relation of mysticism to the utopian tradition, with that tradition being interpreted in a fresh and expanded way. Thus, Ronald Knox's *Enthusiasm* can be read alongside studies of the Dead Sea Scriptures, of Hasidism, of California's utopian colonies, of the histories of communistic and socialist groups, and of more traditional accounts of the teachings of the mystics.

e. Participation in the practice as an essential mode of learning is dramatically illustrated in a winter study program course in "Zen discipline" organized by John Eusden at Williams College. The official description is:

> An exploration of and participation in aspects of Zen Buddhist mind-body training. Students will engage in regular *zazen* (or meditation periods), reading and study, individual projects (e.g., *sumi-e*, haiku poetry, or journal keeping), and in some physical discipline. Trips to Zen centers will be made. Mr. Carl Samuelson, college swimming coach, will assist. A visiting Zen Buddhist master will be present at the beginning of the project.

After two experiences in teaching the course, Eusden observes: "The course began with a problem: 'How to teach a non-Western religion which does not depend on words and verbal communication.' I decided to begin where I had started with Zen in my training and experience at Mioshin-ji Temple in Kyoto in the mid-1960's. All other ways of 'teaching' Zen I now judge as failures, against the fruitfulness of these two attempts.

"For the whole month of January twelve men and women students and three faculty attempt to live the discipline of the Zen way. Our major effort is directed toward authentic *zazen*, meeting regularly as a group at an early morning hour. Individual or private *zazen* is also part of the requirement. Heavy reading assignments are required before the course gets underway, with most of the reading having being finished during Christmas vacation.[10] We do daily mind-body work, dividing the group into cross-country skiers or swimmers. These two sports were chosen because of their similarity to classical Zen body disciplines, such as archery and judo. Cross-country skiing and swimming each use all parts of the body, stress pattern and flow, develop endurance, call for operating in another medium, and encourage relaxation and even the feeling of selflessness. To learn of these qualities in a physical setting is helpful when one tries to practice them in the central discipline of *zazen*.

"We also try to waken entrance into aspects of Zen culture as much as possible (*sumi-e*, or brush and ink drawing, art exhibits, including the unique fabulous show last year at the Boston Fine Arts Museum on 'Zen Paintings and Calligraphy,' tea ceremony). There were field trips to the Zen Studies Center in New York City; and several of our students have spent a great deal of time at Philip Kapleau's Zen Center in Rochester.

"We spent two weekends in concentrated *sesshins* or 'times of collecting thoughts' at a nearby estate owned by the College. On one of these weekends we were joined for part of it by a winter study program in the psychology department which was working on 'The Body and Its Communication.' Interesting parallels and distinctions were drawn and observed by members of both groups.

"Last January over one hundred students wanted to take the course—or rather I should say took the trouble to make an appointment with me to see if they could be in the course. Selectivity was a real problem, but I finally resorted to the Eastern-Western method of random choice. (Not assuming in Zen style that anyone who had read up on, say, Suzuki would be better than someone who had not.)

"The course has become known as the hardest winter study program at Williams. I have never had a more imaginative and perservering response from people at a teaching situation. The experience has radically altered my whole approach to teaching. My spring semester course on religion in American was changed around to include some of the techniques we used in the winter study program."

f. A Psychology of Religion course, developed by William J. Peck at the University of North Carolina, is intended both to be "interdisciplinary in a basic sense" and to engage aspects of the participants' self-understanding.

Following a historical and critical introduction, in which the frustrated development of the psychology of religion and the nature of the discipline as a phase of the problem of religion and culture are treated (readings from Dostoyevsky and William James), the major areas of investigation are:

Personality and the Experience of Chaos (James, Eliade, Zaehner)
  The role of abnormal psychology in religion
  James' concept of the divided self
  Drugs and Mysticism

Personality and Static forms of Order (Freud)
  Moralism and "phariseeism" in religious behavior
  Obsessive-compulsive "mechanisms"
  The role of society and value systems

The Development of Personality (Jung)
  Religious symbolism and the Unconscious
  Jung's idea of the self

Existentialism and the Psychology of Religion (Kierkegaard, Ruitenbeek)
  The issue of self-discovery
  The issue of human freedom

This study is designed to be interdisciplinary by being located at a juncture of several disciplines, including at least depth-psychology, cultural anthropology and theology, with social psychology and sociology as indispensible ancillaries. The conjunction of these approaches makes possible focusing both on problems like conversion and its analogs in ritual initiation, in rapid social change among groups, and in basic cultural transitions at the level of symbol systems.

The course is also directed frankly to "values as an inescapable aspect of the academic task, the definition of the freedom of the person being a value carefully and extensively discussed." This is the "theological dimension." However, an "escape valve" is built into the agreement between teacher and student in that the question of significance for the student's personal religious vision is to be postponed until after the conclusion of the course, so far as possible, and left to individual decision. "No student is to be pressed, beyond his actual readiness, into those aspects of the course having to do with growth and self-understanding. The strictly academic track is always a valid and honorable one for students who do not wish to discuss such personal issues as their dreams and moral quandaries." At the same time the acknowledgement in the classroom of the presence of the "counter culture," and the exploration of its structures, together with the study of thinkers like Freud and Kierkegaard, are designed to engage students deeply "in the search for perspectives which could carry Western man beyond the impasse of culture versus counter culture." The student is seen as a "participant observer," whose own grasp of the issues in the psychology of religion develops out of the struggle with a contemporary model.

g. It is inescapable that this account of more or less radical departures from ordinary course procedures should be concluded with a course entitled "The Meaning of Death," developed by James Carse, New York University. The venture arose in part out of personal interest and partially in response to a change in departmental policy, according to which all traditional "seminary organization" of the subject matter was to be abandoned and courses were to be designed around specific topics. The idea of presenting an adequate survey of the entire field of religion was eschewed, not only because of the small size of the deparment, but also as a way of rejecting the idea (e.g., of Newman), that there is a clear boundary to a subject matter, and that therefore there are ways of ascertaining whether it has been fully covered in the course offering. The result has been a combination of traditional-sounding courses and some reasonably innovative departures, involving those aspects of religion which are most interesting to members of the department and in which they are currently involved in scholarship.

Congruently, the intention of the course on death was not to present a comprehensive coverage of the meaning of death "in all ages and places," nor to argue for any particular view, but rather "to provide students with what was called in the course syllabus 'points of departure' (no pun intended) for students to enter into their own reflection on the nature of death." Students (in large numbers) came with a wide range of "existential" interests, as well as (in some cases) out of a judgment that this was a "freaky subject that was great to discuss while stoned or tripping." The mood and spirit of the course was "both relaxed and intense, academic and personal." Few students were interested in exploring questions of the survival after death.

Because of the deep personal involvement of most participants, departures from ordinary pedagogical patterns were obviously in order. Lectures, frequently by guests, were used, covering topics such as euthenasia, sociological patterns of dying in the United States and views of death in numerous religious traditions. Much more important in generating discussion and reflection were videotapes and films (e.g., "El Topo," "An Occurrence at Owl Creek Bridge," "Ordet" and special events (e.g., an interview of terminal patients in a New York hospital).

Informal discussions meetings in the instructor's home and

other places around Washington Square were extremely well attended and usually intensely personal, several times verging into "consciousness-raising sessions." Carse comments: "I was somewhat concerned that the general tone of the course, and particularly the discussions, remain slightly cool. I had thought that there was some hazard in spending so much time, and so intensely on the subject of death. This was confirmed by many students who felt that the discussions approached the danger point several times."

The heart of the class for most students proved to be the single assigned project: the presentation to the class of a verbal or non-verbal "personal statement" of the meaning of death. No limitation was placed on the nature of the project, but only the condition that if it was non-verbal or creative, rather than a statement in the form of a term paper, the author or poet or sculptor or dancer would have to be willing to perform or display his work before the other members of the class. (It may be evidence of the deep personal involvement that all refused to perform before the entire class, so that these were scheduled for evenings in the instructor's apartment.) The results ranged "from a videotape of an autopsy to blasting multimedia performances of virtuosic achievement and little literal reference to death itself." Because of the intensely personal character of the assignment it was agreed that the grade for all personal statements would be B's, except in cases where they were clearly inadequate in which case the grade would be C. For those students for whom the grade of A was important, an informal oral examination was arranged at the end of the semester covering the reading assignments and the material in the lectures.

A class of this sort, as Carse comments, raises a number of problems that may be shared by others who attempt to deal academically with "existential" subjects. Not the least of these is the discovery of an appropriate format for preserving critical distance while respecting the depth of student concerns. "There is something about the subject matter that resists the idea of a course and lectures; however, by the same account, the subject is so intensely personal that about the only safe way to approach it is via an objective academic course structure which I attempted to preserve to the end." Another is the problem of evaluation in a course that centers around a personal statement, whose content cannot be evaluated in the fact that it is a *personal* statement. Here sympathetic listening was more often an appropriate stance on the part of the instructor. The instructor "can only nod, feel and behold." A course can be for that reason of greatest importance to many students, and it can be a cheap credit for others. When the entire responsibility of thought is thrown on the student, the instructor risks manipulation of his trust, but the risk must be taken. Finally, in this instance, the question arises whether a more modest time span would be better. If the subject of death "is too deep and

122

confusing to deal with in one or two lectures of a course on another subject," it may at the same time be "too deep and confusing to spend an entire course on it. Maybe half a semester would have been better."

6. Notes Toward a Conclusion

It is not the purpose of this volume to be perscriptive. The appropriate conclusion should therefore point mainly to unresolved issues. The brief reflections and questions that follow grow particularly out of the preceding sketches in Part III, though they look back also to the position papers in Part I.

1. The options—sometimes dilemmas—faced in religious studies exist at all levels of the academic enterprise, from the classroom to the institution as a whole. The choices are prima facie pedagogical, relating to courses and programs, but they rest essentially on broader decisions, concerning questions not at all peculiar to religious studies, questions such as "What is liberal education?" "What is academic responsibility?" "What are the goals of contemporary public, private and church-related institutions of higher learning?" The questions for religious studies thus merge increasingly with the questions of liberal education generally, and if the goals and patterns of the former are unclear it is largely because the aims and norms of undergraduate education as a whole are uncertain.

2. For all undergraduate education, a major issue is the balancing of concern and commitment with the criteria and standards of empirical or scientific investigation. In religious studies, this issue has its focus in the explicit concern of religion with ultimacy and with life-commitment, hence the unavoidability of questions of advocacy and self-criticism. Because of this, the study of religion may be a singularly useful illustration of the universal problems of involvement vs. disengagement. Within the framework of traditional and nearly universal standards such as thoroughness, honesty and consideration of all available evidence, how wide can the range of responsible decisions extend ? - to the outright exclusion of theologizing (compare political theory)? or to the open embrace of advocacy (political action)?

3. How can the traditional areas of study (e.g., scriptural studies, history of Christianity) not only make room for but adopt new ways of doing things? If the questions were merely the former, we should simply expect increasing displacement of the traditional subject-areas by new objects of study and definitions of the field. But there is evidence of significant efforts to redefine the objects and purposes of the old—for example, such that courses legitimately titled, "History of Christianity" become also means to contemporary reflection on the contemporary.

4. To what extent should student interest and "demand" be allowed to govern the contour of courses and curricula? What happens if student demand (e.g., for a "guru," for "relevance") runs counter to the presumed demands of academic responsibility? Why should the study of religion face this issue any more than history or literature?

5. Given the growing preoccupation with methodological problems, what are the most fruitful ways of teaching the methods for the study of religion? How can these be integrated with "subject-matter" content in undergraduate courses? And how can methodological considerations be disengaged from their theoretical "Ueberbau" and be communicated as practical recipes for investigation that can actually be followed and applied by students? In other words, how can one learn how to study religion?

6. There is a considerable measure of agreement on new (and desirable) directions in the study of religion: for example, cross-cultural and interdisciplinary studies, concern with contemporary (including non-traditional) forms of religious experience, the use of new "scriptures" (movies, novels, etc.) and the study of non-Western religions. Are there educational rationales which would exclude these developments on principle (e.g., institutional religious commitments)? Or are the problems of lag in implementation essentially structural and practical (e.g., departmental and institutional organization)?

7. What is the special academic and/or historical responsibility of the church-related institution to its particular religious tradition? How does this responsibility differ (if at all) from that of public and private institutions that deal with the same or similar material, e.g., Catholic or biblical theology: What criteria of academic responsibility may be seen as universal and neutral, no matter what the educational goals of an institution?

8. "Participative" courses raise sharply the problem of defining new criteria for academic responsibility, both of faculty and students. Just which interest group(s) in the academic and public domains can and/or should legislate such criteria? Can the line between critical analysis and self-discovery be drawn? Is there any single set of norms for determining the academic quality of a course or a program? What counts as a violation of these norms, i.e., as an alleged instance of inferiority? If objectives are redefined, what are appropriate criteria for ascertaining whether the objectives are attained?

9. Religious studies faces a special problem of defining and interpreting an undergraduate major. What is it "for," or is it "for" anything,—apart from preparation for graduate studies? Since the study of religion must deal with "objective" knowledge or subject matter, as well as knowledge about oneself, which may or may not be an incidental result of any course, what is it that a religion major should be expected to *know*? But again, does the study of religion involve any problem here that is not at the same time a question for modern drama, or poetry or ethics of sociology, or for undergraduate education as a whole?

---

[1]*This has perhaps been less true in Catholic colleges that build on parochial school education. The growth of the study of religion in the public secondary schools may of course sharply alter the situation.*

[2]*In several of these formulations, I have drawn on a privately circulated paper by Roland Delattre (of the University of Tennessee), on "The Problem of the Introductory Course."*

[3]*This introductory course is paralleled by another, somewhat more traditional pattern, a course in "Judaism, Roman Catholicism and Protestantism," designed to appeal to the interests of undergraduates who want especially to know something more about the three major religious traditions in the United States. It does not, however, follow the common historical approach, but seeks to raise key questions concerning writings, worship, leaders, religious community, and the relationship of the religious community and the world.*

[4]*There is also a major offered in the Department of Religious Education, as well as several "practical" degrees offered through that department, e.g., B.S. in Religious Education and Secretarial Science, and B.S. in Religious Education and Business Administration.*

[5]*Some courses are available in others of the Claremont Colleges.*

[6]*For a discussion of those issues, see K. Bridston and D. Culver, Pre-Seminary Education (Minneapolis, 1965).*

[7]*The following summary is based on a report by chairman Nicholas Piediscalzi.*

[8]*The description draws on a statement by Luther H. Martin, Jr. and William Paden.*

[9]*The details, with fuller reflections on the values of the procedures, are more fully given in the Bulletin of the Council on the Study of Religion, Vol. 2, No. 1, February 1971.*

[10]Readings included N. W. Ross, The World of Zen; Z. Shibayama, A Flower Does Not Talk: Zen Essays; F. Spiegelberg, Zen, Rocks, and Waters; D. T. Suzuki, Zen and Japanese Culture; Stewart, ed., A Net of Fireflies, Haiku for the Seasoned; P. Wienpahl, The Matter of Zen, and A Zen Diary; H. Doumulin, A History of Zen Buddhism; W. Johnston, The Still Point: Reflections on Zen and Christian Mysticism; and Boston Museum of Fine Arts, Zen Paintings and Calligraphy: Catalog and Commentary.

SELECTED
BIBLIOGRAPHY

Bellah, Robert. "Confessions of a Former Establishment Fundamentalist," *Bulletin of the Council on the Study of Religion* (CSR, 1970), Vol. 1, no. 3, p. 3.

Cutler, Alan. "Memo Concerning the Ideal Type of Program in Religious Studies for a Great Research Oriented University," *Bulletin of the American Academy of Religion* (AAR, 1968), Vol. V, no. 3, p. 2. Grandiose scheme of a history-oriented religion department suggests that greatness may reside in the number (38 altogether) and scholarly detachment of the faculty.

Hartzell, Karl, and Harrison Sasscer. *The Study of Religion in the Campus Today: Selected Papers from the Stony Brook Conference in Religion as an Academic Discipline.* (Washington: Association of America Colleges, 1967) Some cogent critiques of why and how religion is studied as an "academic discipline." Also reviews the philosophy of departmentalization, cross-disciplinary study, values in liberal education, faculty representation, etc.

Harvey, Van A. "Reflections on the Study of Religion," *Journal of the American Academy of Religion* (AAR, 1970), Vol. XXXVIII, no. 1, p. 17-29. Autobiography and history are combined in reviewing the question: From seminary to university—now where?

Hauer, Christian. "Religion and Interdisciplinary Inquiry: Are the Prospects Changing?" *Bulletin of the American Academy of Religion* (AAR, 1968), Vol. V., no. 3, p. 6. Offers some impressionistic explanations why religion faculty in particular tend to engage in interdisciplinary programs.

Holbrook, Clyde. *Religion, A Humanistic Field.* (Englewood Cliffs, N.J.: Prentice-Hall, 1963)

Johnson, Dale. "Freshman Religion Course—Luther College," *Bulletin of the American Academy of Religion* (AAR, 1967), Vol. IV, no. 3, p. 5. Brief account of an introductory course, which utilizes cross-disciplinary procedures. The course constitutes (with English and History) nearly 50% of the average freshman's course-load.

Livingston, James. "Criteria for Organizing the Introductory Course in Religion," *Bulletin of the Council on the Study of Religion* (CSR, 1971) Vol. 2, no. 3, p. 8. Criteria: methodology, broad patterns of religious response, cross-cultural and trans-temporal material used as explanation, engagement of student.

McLean, Milton. *Religious Studies in Public Universities.* (Carbondale, Illinois: Southern Illinois University, 1967) A series of essays considers the reasons for and the forms of change in the post-War growth of religion study in state supported higher education. Also included are brief descriptions of religion programs in 135 institutions, with catalogue (1965-1967) exhibits of 24 public and private university religion departments.

Michaelsen, Robert. "The Scholarly Study of Religion in College and University," (New Haven, Society for Religion in Higher Education, 1964) An essay reviewing the rather limited philosophy of education, curriculum situation, and historical milieu, just prior to the rapid expansion of religious studies in the latter half of the '60's.

_____. *The Study of Religion in American Universities:Ten Case Studies With Special Reference to State Universities*. New Haven: The Society for Religion in Higher Education, 1965.

_____. "The Study of Religion:A Quiet Revolution in American University," in Milton McLean (ed.), *Religious Studies in Public Universities*. Carbondale, Ill.: Southern Illinois University, 1967. Documents the growth of student interest in and institutional adaptation to the study of religion, particularly in the public and private sector in the early to mid '60's.

_____. *Piety in the Public Schools: Trends and Issues in the Relationship Between Religion and the Public Schools in the U.S.* New York: Macmillan, 1970. Legal and religious background of church-state separation. Well-documented history, includes pertinent Supreme Court decisions.

Neusner, Jacob. "Do Others Face This Problem," *Bulletin of the American Academy of Religion* (AAR, 1967), Vol. XXXV, no. 1, p. 11. Presents the dilemma of the historically honest professor of religion confronted by the student's personal need to believe.

_____. "What to Do About Judaism," *Bulletin of the American Academy of Religion* (AAR, 1967), Vol. IV, no. 3, p. 10. Useful syllabus and remarks on the problem of teaching Judaism. (cf. *ibid.*, Vol. V, no. 1, p. 21 for bibliography.) (cf. *ibid.* Vol. V, no. 2, p. 8 for conclusion of "What to Do About Judaism.")

Ramsey, Paul, and John F. Wilson, editors. *The Study of Religion in Colleges and Universities*. Princeton: Princeton University Press, 1970. One of the best issue-oriented statements to date.

Shepherd, William. "Religion and the Counter Culture: A New Religiosity," (unpublished—to be published in *Sociological Inquiry*, with replies from Bellah, Baum and Lidz.) A discussion of youthful existentialism:youth without "truth-claims."

Slater, C. P. "An Introductory Religion Course," *Bulletin of the American Academy of Religion* (AAR, 1967), Vol. XXXV, no. 2, p. 17.

Sloyan, Gerard. "The New Role of the Study of Religion in Higher Education:What Does It Mean?", *Journal of Ecumenical Studies*, Vol. VI, (1969), pp. 1-17. Using Catholic institutions as the main example, the author asks whether theology and religious practice still have a role in the university. Contrasts traditional religion with the new religion of "academic study."

Smart, Ninian. "Religion as a Subject," *The Church Quarterly*, Vol. II (1970), pp. 227ff.

_____. "Religious Studies at Lancaster, England" *Council on the Study of Religious Bulletin* (CSR, 1971), Vol. 2, no. 3. p. 3. An American style department in a new British University. Raises some issues and rationales for curricular revision.

Smith, Huston. "The Interdepartmental Approach to Religious Studies," *Journal of Higher Education*, Vol. XXXI, (1960), p. 5ff.

Smith, Wilfred Cantwell. "The Study of Religion and the Study of the Bible," *Journal of the American Academy of Religion* (AAR, 1971), Vol. XXXIX, no. 2, p. 131. An imaginative reconception of biblical studies. Outline of an undergraduate course that investigates the role of the Bible in Western history, rather than that of salvation history in the Bible.

Spivey, Robert. "Modest Messiahs: The Study of Religion in State Universities," *Religious Education*, Vol. LXIII, no. 1, (1968) p. 5ff. Public university scholarship as omen for the entire field of religious studies. Use of University of North Carolina and Florida State as examples.

Sullivan, William J. "The Academic Study of Religion in Catholic Colleges and Universities," *College Newsletter*, National Catholic Education Association, Vol. XXXIII, no. 4, 1971. Theology as religious study. Catholic tradition compatible with intellectual honesty. Curricular inclusion of "commitment" and "descriptive" courses.

Thompson, Henry. "A Reply to Dr. Neusner: 'On the Personal Dimension of Academic Religion'," *Bulletin of the American Academy of Religion* (AAR, 1967), Vol. IV, no. 3, p. 7.

Underwood, Kenneth. *The Church, the University, and Social Policy*, (The Danforth Study of Campus Ministries.) Vol. 1: Report of the Director. (Middletown, Connecticut:Wesleyan University Press, 1969)

_____. "Is the Lecture Method Dead." *Bulletin of the American Academy of Religion (AAR, 1967) Vol. XXXV, No. 2, p. 17. (Early) experiments with audio and visual alternatives to the lecture.*

Welch, Claude. *Graduate Education in Religion: A Critical Appraisal.* Missoula, Montana: University of Montana Press, 1971.

_____. "Identity Crisis in the Study of Religion? A First Report on the ACLS Study," *Journal of the American Academy of Religion* (AAR, 1971) Vol. XXXIX, No. 1, p. 3.

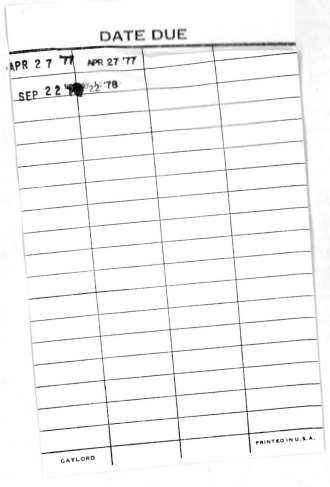